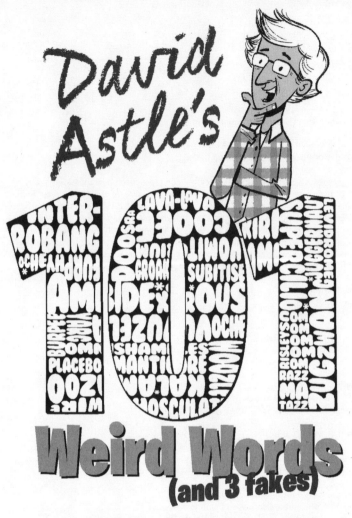

David Astle's

101

Weird Words
(and 3 fakes)

From Ambidextrous to Zugzwang

with illustrations by Paul Tippett

T0116571

First published by Allen & Unwin in 2018

Allen & Unwin
83 Alexander Street
Crows Nest NSW 2065
Australia
Phone: (61 2) 8425 0100
Email: info@allenandunwin.com
Web: www.allenandunwin.com

A catalogue record for this book is available from the National Library of Australia

ISBN 978 176063 366 0

For teaching resources, explore
www.allenandunwin.com/resources/for-teachers

Cover and text design by Sandra Nobes
Set in 10.5 pt Corbert Condensed by Sandra Nobes
This book was printed in October 2018 by McPherson's Printing Group, Australia.

10 9 8 7 6 5 4 3 2 1

www.davidastle.com

The paper in this book is FSC® certified.
FSC® promotes environmentally responsible, socially beneficial and economically viable management of the world's forests.

INTRODUCTION

Can you **groak**? Do you know a **lava-lava** from a **muu-muu**? Have you ever seen a **chatoyant kalamazoo** in a **vomitorium**?

Here's the book to help you know, one way or the other.

Soon we zoom from **ambidextrous** to **zugzwang**, meeting weirdness at every turn. Some words you will know already, but not the secrets they hide. Other words you may not know, like **risley** or **rhopalic**, **quidnunc** or **glabella**, but all four are worth meeting, believe me.

Soon you'll bump into **belladonna** and **levidrome**, plus a hundred other astounding words, discovering what they mean and how they ended up in English. (Warning: some stories involve smelly cheese and old undies.) There's a helpful guide to pronouncing each oddity, too.

You can also play detective, snooping out my three fake words hiding among the hundred and one others. It won't be easy, but see if you can spot them.

Then again, if you prefer to know which words are real and which are phony, take a peek at the last page. Or check there when your detective work is done. I bet you won't score three out of three!

More than a dictionary, more than a mystery, *101 Weird Words (and 3 Fakes)* is also a book abounding in mini-puzzles, corny riddles and cool word-facts, not to mention Paul's zany pictures.

What more do you need? Time to get wordy. Get weird. And get reading.

AMBIDEXTROUS
[AM-bee-DEX-truss]

Put up both hands if you know what **AMBIDEXTROUS** means. That's right – ambidextrous people are **skilled with both hands**.

Cooks who pick their nose with either left or right forefingers are ambidextrous. Same goes for footballers who kick with either foot. Hands or feet – it doesn't matter which extremity, so long as you're handy on both sides.

Speaking of sides, look what happens when AMBIDEXTROUS is cut in half. See anything amazing?

AMBIDE / XTROUS

To spot the secret, count the vowels. All five are there, but that's not the coolest part. Because AMBIDEXTROUS has twelve **unique letters**, not one repeat. So why split the word in two? As a clue, think about the alphabet.

Can you see the secret? Here we go: AMBIDE – the word's first half – uses six letters from the alphabet's first half. Then comes XTROUS – the second half, a set of six letters from the alphabet's other half. Believe it or not, ambidextrous is ambidextrous!

 Jugglers juggle AMBIDEXTROUSLY, one more spectacular word – fourteen letters with no letter repeated!

AMOSNIAC
[ay-MOZ-nee-ACK]

Every summer, I turn into
a blood bank. My customers
are mosquitoes, who visit all
hours of the night, jabbing my
arms and legs for more business.

I'm quite the buzz with mosquitoes;
my blood is the tastiest in the street.

How I wish to be an **AMOSNIAC**, a person whose
blood doesn't delight those little suckers. Camping trips
would be twice the fun with no jabs or scabs to pester
me.

Mosquito comes from *musca* in Latin, their word for
fly. And when I say fly I mean the bug, not the zip or
the art of wagging your wings mid-air. Mosquito in fact
means **little fly**, despite both bugs flying in separate
clouds.

But give me flies any day of the week, or any night.
I'm not fussy. Flies are a picnic compared to a mozzie
swarm. Sure, flies are annoying but mosquitoes really
needle me. Are you a blood bank or an amosniac?

Find the right rhyme for each word below and you
can reveal a creepy mozzie fact.

AUSSIES BAN PINK TREE LIMES WHERE SKATE FIN MUD.

Mozzies can drink three times their weight in blood.

4

AMPERSAND

[*AM-purr-sand*]

Fish & chips are delicious, especially with a sprinkle of salt & vinegar.

Did you gobble that last sentence easily? I bet you did, because the **AMPERSAND** is part & parcel of modern writing.

Like an awkward 8 with a cute twin-tail, the ampersand is better known as the **and-symbol**. Ampersand is short for **and per se**, meaning **and by itself**, one doodle doing the work of a common word, just as **@** means **at**, or **$** is **dollar**.

The ampersand has been around for over two thousand years. Graffiti on the walls of Pompeii, a town buried by volcanic ash, is full of ampersands – at least the early version of the emblem. Rather than a wonky 8, the symbol resembled this:

Ampersands are popular in brand names too, making them easier to squeeze onto signs & labels. Plenty of passwords include ampersands as well, the curly squiggle a dollop of mystery to sit amid the usual letters & numbers.

Before emojis ruled the web, there were things called **emoticons**, faces built with keyboard symbols. For example, **:-(** was the modern 😦, while **:-&** was the emoticon for tongue-tied 😝.

ARCHAEOPTERYX

[ahr-kee-OPP-tuh-riks]

Remember this word – it might crop up in a spelling bee. Remember this bird too, because it's a **flying dinosaur**.

Wait, you say. Was is it a reptile or a bird? And I say, why not both? The **ARCHAEOPTERYX** was a living marvel on two legs, a flapper from the fossil age.

Split in two, *archaeo* is Greek for **old**, while *pteryx* means **wing**, this old bird owning the oldest wings in the west.

The animal boasted feathers as well. Way back in 1860, a German palaeontologist named Hermann von Meyer found a feather imprinted in limestone. His skin went cold. His heart raced. What was he looking at? It felt bizarre, seeing a random quill existing in a quarry littered with dinosaur bones.

Soon after, the archaeopteryx was celebrated as the link between reptiles and birds. Barely longer than a ruler, this archaeopteryx once ruled the Jurassic skies – a killer canary before canaries were hatched.

 Q: What do you call a fossil that never lifts a finger?

A: Lazybones

AWRY

[uh-RYE]

What's happening?! Why is *this sentence going* **AWRY**?

Awry means **crooked**, or **crookedly**. If you button your shirt the wrong way, tucking every button into holes where they don't belong, then your buttons are awry because you buttoned awry.

To make matters worse, if you think awry rhymes with **story**, or **glory**, then sorry – you're saying awry awry. Why? Because awry rhymes with **a lie**, and that's the truth.

Awry comes from **wry**, while wry comes from *wrigian* – the old English for **bend**. Heaps of bendy words begin with WR, like **wriggle** and **wrist**, **wring** and **wrap**, **wrench** and **writhe**. Add the A to WRY, and that makes the word mean 'on the wrong way' or 'in the wrong direction', like when your basketball lob goes awry of the hoop.

Before we go, awry has nothing to do with awe, which means **fear** or **wonder**. Like I wonder why my words here are still going awry? Of course, that's it! How awesome – I'm wryting!

 Q: Which African beast is bent?

BELLADONNA

[BELL-ah-DON-ah]

If you want to live a long and happy life, skip this word. Go straight to BOOTLEG over the page and keep on reading. Please. I won't mind.

Still here? Be warned. Because one spoonful of **BELLADONNA** in your muesli, and you'll choke. One smidgen on your lips and you'll keel over, flapping about like a landed trout.

The poison's full name is *Atropa belladonna*, a substance squeezed from a shaggy green plant called **deadly nightshade** – not the sort of greenery to toss into a salad.

Years ago, doctors used belladonna to numb patients for surgery. Too big a dose and the patient would die. Too little and they'd feel every cut and scrape. Life was short back then. Short and experimental.

Belladonna was also found in eyedrops, the poison perfect for widening a woman's pupils. Bigger eyes somehow made a maiden a *bella donna* (or **beautiful woman**, in Italian). Peculiar to think a deadly sap, once plinked into an eyeball, is named after a compliment.

 According to English folklore, witches mixed belladonna, poppy juice and hemlock to make a special soaring potion. Please, don't fly this at home.

BOOTLEG
[BOOT-leg]

Horsehair can get scratchy, rubbing against a rider's skin all day. That's why most riders wear long boots, to protect their legs.

High as the knee, the boots happen to be tailor-made for concealing things. Things like bottles in particular, their shape and size just right for snuggling. Brilliant for smuggling too, hiding the bottles from nosy people. Riders in America discovered this tactic last century, using their boots to stash wine and whisky bottles behind the leather. Back then, like now, you could only drink such drinks if you paid tax to the state.

To protect this law, police searched riders' pockets for any undercover alcohol. They checked saddles and carts and luggage, but no luck. All this time the booze was in those tall boots.

Soon **BOOTLEG** became slang for **anything made or bought against the law**. Now you find bootleg DVDs or bootleg handbags or even bootleg boots – any item slyly sold where the state doesn't get a cent.

 Q: What is a horse's favourite sport?

A: Stable tennis

BORBORYGMUS

[*bawr-buh-RIG-muhs*]

Maybe you ate your salami sandwich too fast. Or you drank so many long gulps of juice your stomach can't cope.

How can you tell? Those groans from below, that rumble in your guts, is how your stomach speaks without using words.

Next time that happens, or your friend's tummy turns talkative, just say, 'Shhhh – I can hear some **BORBORYGMUS**.'

'What?' they ask.

'You're bellowing above the belt.'

Borborygmus is a doctor's term for the drastic gastric racket, the tummy rumble spelling trouble. The word was burped into life by old Greeks, trying to echo their belly's inner noise. Say the syllables slowly and you mimic a guzzle-guts in agony.

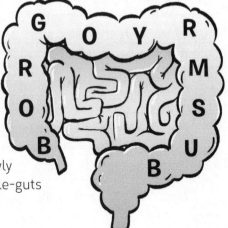

Q: What belly fluff is delicious?

BRIO
[*BREE-oh*]

BRIO means a splash of energy, a dash of dash.

Think **pep**. Think **vibrant**. If you dance with **flair**, then you dance with brio. English is teeming with words of energy, from **zeal** to **zest**, from **vim** to **verve**, from **gusto** to **get-up-and-go**. But the best in this dynamic word-fest is brio.

The minute Italians invented brio, we wanted it. Needed it. Stole it. Musicians will know brio from score sheets, where a melody played *con brio* (**with lively energy**) means a truckload of sparkling sound.

As a game, say brio aloud. Louder! What a sound, like gooey brie cheese meeting an O-shaped bagel, or a summer breeze interrupted by a sigh. Like a word too happy to finish, the speaker so distracted by the joy of life that the beautiful O-sound floats away like a party balloon.

😊 **Relish** is a type of sauce, as well as another word for joy. When you do something with brio, you do it with relish. So what saucy Mexican snack owns this letter pattern?

B _ R _ I _ O

Burrito – which means little donkey!

BRUSQUE
[*BRUSK*]

Say I turned weepy while watching a sad movie. Being my friend, if you felt **BRUSQUE**, then you might say: 'Deal with it, David. Life can be glum. Movies are nothing but made-up stories, and you need to get over it.'

Gee, thanks a lot. Call yourself a friend? You're almost being rude, but not fully. Brusque is how we describe someone whose manner is too direct. **Curt** is another word we might use. So is **blunt**, when a speaker neglects to consider how others might feel.

Brusque is connected to an old Italian broom. Picture a swisher made of sticks, with a homemade handle and twigs for bristles. Now picture a butcher sweeping his sawdust out the door and you get the right action in your mind.

In ancient Italian, that broom is a *bruscus*, a tool to chase off grime and dust, just as you swept away my tears, you brusque person, you. That movie was so sad. Don't you have a heart?!

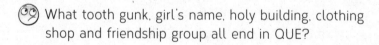 What tooth gunk, girl's name, holy building, clothing shop and friendship group all end in QUE?

Plaque, Monique, mosque, boutique, clique

BURPEE
[BURP-ee]

Stand with your hands by your side. Now squat low. Next, plant your palms on the ground and then kick your feet behind you, turning your body into a plank, your belly hovering above the floor.

Hold it! Hold it! Now kick your feet back into the squat position. And last thing, stand up, just as you started.

Congratulations – you just did a **BURPEE**, a word that triggers giggles every time I hear it. Because if a person who burps is a **burper**, then is the hearer of the burp a **burpee**?

Not if you ask a man called Royal Burpee. Promise you, that was his real name. Royal was a health freak from New York who designed this exercise eighty years ago. Push-ups and sit-ups needed a fix-up, he thought, bringing the burpee into life, just like a lemonade drinker can bring a burp to life.

BUR (or burr) is a pod that sticks to your socks. PEE is a letter or a tinkle. Together they make BURPEE. Can you pair these others to make eight more words? CAR + PET, say, is CARPET. Words come from any column, but can only be used once.

CAR	DAM	DEN	EON
FAT	FOR	FUR	HER
MAT	PEN	PET	PIG
PUT	RID	ROW	WAR

Carpet, dampen, father, format, furrow, pigeon, putrid, warden

BURQINI
[bur-KEE-nee]

Burqa can be spelt burka, or burqua, or burkah, or burkha, plus a few more ways just for fun.

The dictionary gives us so many choices because Arabic ignores our A-B-C stuff, inviting English translators to capture the Arabic word in sound, using letters.

Burqa is the Arabic dress that flows as freely as Arabic script. Made of light fabric, the burqa covers the body from head to toe. Many Muslim women wear burqas in public as part of their faith.

The full burqa includes the **hijab** – or headscarf – and the **niqab** – a face veil. Great words, aren't they – burqa, hijab and niqab? I love seeing Q free of U, like a letter running loose of its shadow.

But in summer, when temperatures climb, a swim gets hard to resist. One pool plunge and your body cools down. Not so easy if you need your skin covered and most cozzies at the swim-shop are scanty.

This problem was solved by Australian designer Aheda Zanetti. Herself a Muslim, Aheda crafted the **BURQINI** in 2016, combining the **burqa** with the **bikini**, offering a chance to splash among the waves without a flesh flash.

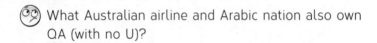 What Australian airline and Arabic nation also own QA (with no U)?

QANTAS, Qatar

CACOPHONY

[kuh-KOF-uh-nee]

A **hammer** makes a **clamour**. Add ten more hammers, and pick a few picks, and you make a **CACOPHONY**, a raucous word for **racket**.

And should one hammer jam your thumb, causing you to yowl a chorus of ows, then the whole cacophony verges on **catastrophe**!

Cacophony comes from two Greek words joining forces. *Caco* is the old word for **bad**, or **gross**, sitting next to **phony**, the real result of *phonos* – or **sound**.

A ruckus, a rumpus – cacophony is a gross string of noises, the ear-splitting opposite of harmony. Car alarms make a cacophony. Same for squeaky brakes, a dentist's drill or a fine violin played un-finely.

Ask some people and they might say rock music is **cacophonic**. It all depends what *phonos* you prefer in your earphones. One person's melody is another listener's cacophony.

 Q: What band plays whale music?

A: An orca-stra

CAPTCHA
[KAP-chuh]

CAPTCHA is a **trap built to capture robots** on the internet.

But before we go further, notice how CAPTCHA keeps its **capital letters** all the way down the page, unlike every other word in this book so far.

That's because each letter in CAPTCHA stands for another word. LOL does the same trick, short for Laughing Out Loud. Yet most people write **lol** these days, those three letters shrinking into lower-case.

CAPTCHA is still too young for that to happen. The seven initials stand for Completely Automated Public Turing test to tell Computers and Humans Apart.

Turing was the London-born maths wizard who inspired this computer test. CAPTCHA is a gizmo guarding heaps of websites, asking visitors to copy warped letters into a field, or maybe select candles from a panel of candles and pencils. Only humans can do that, not machines, thus keeping the spam robots away.

 You might know NERF balls as spongy toys you can throw without breaking windows. NERF stands for Non-Expanding Recreational Foam.

CHATOYANT

[*shah-TOY-ant*]

CHATOYANT sounds divine long before you know its lavish meaning. Check out that spelling and you may spy a **toy** wrapped inside a **chant**, like some kind of Kinder Surprise.

Chant *shah-TOY-ant* and you'll fall even deeper in love. So musical, so melodic, but the genuine surprise is what the word means.

Do you have any silk in your house? What about a cat? Both things are chatoyant, having the power to change colour as they move.

The word is French, meaning **to gleam like a cat's eye**. Next time you go for a drive, look for those red circles on poles, small red buttons we call cat's eyes. They were produced by a cyclist called Percy Shaw, a cyclist from an English place called **West Riding**!

Percy was sick of crashing his bike after sundown, so he toyed with glass to make reflectors. He called them cat's eyes, as real cat's eyes shine when you flash a torch their way. Shine and change their gleam, in that wondrous chatoyant fashion.

 One of the most chatoyant gems in the world is a yellowy quartz called a tiger's eye. Purrfect.

COOEE
[KOO-ee]

If you ever get lost, then yell **COOEE** at the top of your lungs.

Lost in a major way, I mean. Like stuck in the bush where you can't see your family or friends, not lost at the mall for thirty-three seconds. If that happens, stay where you are, or find the help desk. Yelling cooee in a juice bar is the opposite of cool.

Mobile phones didn't exist in the days of Captain Cook, the era when cooee entered English. The Dharug people of Sydney first hooted this holler over the valleys, the two sharp syllables guaranteed to carry across the harbour, signalling hello to a mate, or confessing they were lost.

Over a hundred years ago, a troop of young farmers marched to Sydney, cooeeing as they walked. With each cooee they hoped other farmers might join them. The group was keen to go to war, using the Cooee March to attract more soldiers.

If you live near your school, then your school is **within cooee**. Another way of saying **close by**, it means the playground is in yelling distance of your place – in case you ever lose your way.

Q: Why did Little Bo Peep go cooee?

A: She'd lost her whey.

CURGLAFF
[KERR-glaf]

Scotland has three mysteries:

1) The Loch Ness Monster. Is there really an underwater Godzilla below the surface of Loch Ness, a chilly lake up north?
2) Underwear. In particular the undies a man wears under his kilt. What's that tartan skirt hiding, and why do people keep asking?
3) If you live in a cold place like Scotland, why would you run a cold bath?

We know about this third mystery due to **CURGLAFF**, a Scottish-English word for the shock your bum feels when first **dipping into cold water**.

Why, Scotland, why? Warm up your water! Or turn down your cold! (That's the green-coloured tap on the right.) Curglaff is a Gaelic word, a mix of **unpleasant** (*cur*) and **moment** (*glaff*).

No question, plunking your bottom in icy Scottish water would be one unpleasant moment. That Loch Ness Monster is welcome to it.

Other cur-words in Gaelic are **curfuggle** (knot of hair), **curbawdy** (looking for an argument) and **curnawin** (burning hunger).

DIK-DIK

[DIK-dik]

Quiet! You need to shush if you wish to spot a
DIK-DIK ambling over the plain. Soaking up the African
sun, this **dwarfish antelope** loves to munch leaves
and berries on low branches.

The branches need be low because the dik-dik is
short, the male a few centimetres shorter than the
female.

Come breeding time, the dik-diks pair for life.
Together, Mr and Mrs Dik-Dik mark their grazing patch
with poo, dropping dung across the plain to explain to
other dik-diks *we don't want visitors, thank you very
much. Text or emails only if you must.*

Despite that strategic poo, intruders still come,
creatures with big teeth and sharp claws. Predators
like lions and cheetahs, hyenas and hawks. Half the
savannah, in fact, love devouring dik-diks.

Dik-dik, the name, comes from this antelope's noise,
a shrill click only the females utter when those
intruders visit. Dik-dik the sound is dik-dik dialect for
yikes-yikes. Let's scram.

 Do you know an extinct bird whose name, like
dik-dik, consists of two repeated sounds?

Dodo

DISCOMBOBULATE

[*dis-kuhm-BOB-yuh-layt*]

Als de taal in een boek overschakelt van het Engels naar een taal die u niet kent, dan zullen de vreemde woorden verbijsterend zijn.

Have I lost you? Let me translate:

If the language in a book switches from English to a language you don't know, then the strange words will **DISCOMBOBULATE.**

The opening language is Dutch. Did you recognise it? Or did the words bewilder? Discombobulate is a wilder brother of **bewilder**, a more confounding word for **confuse**.

The word was dreamt up in the 1830s, a zany American word aiming to sound smart or funny, or maybe both at once. Around the 1830s, the dictionary also added **absquatulate** (to go) and **spifflicate** (to hit), two more words bound to discombobulate.

Look carefully. Discombobulate holds the ingredients of **disturb** and **confound** and **frustrate** – all those things that muddle the mind, the verbs to inspire every human 'Huh?'

 Q: When is a yoyo confused?

 A: When it's thrown for a loop.

25

DOOSRA
[DOOZ-rah]

Keen cricket players know about the **DOOSRA**. Though not every cricketer can *hit* a doosra, a wily delivery a bowler might bowl. Good luck guessing which way it will bounce!

Doosra comes from Urdu, the chief language of Pakistan. It means **the other one**, as that's what Moin Khan – Pakistan's wicketkeeper of the 1990s – kept yelling to Saqlain Mushtaq, the spinner who invented this doozy of a delivery.

'Doosra!' begged Khan. 'Doosra, Saqlain!'*

Training in the nets, Saqlain found a way to send the ball left, skimming along the edge of the bat. Spin it the right way and the doosra will catch the batter off-guard, as fielders catch the batter's bungled shot.

وہ امپائر کیسا ہے**

Not too many English words own the pair SR. **Disrupt** and **disregard** are two. **Misread** is another one. But what SR-word is a place designed for schoolkids?

---

* 'Please, Saqlain. Bowl the other one – you know, the ball that bounces the opposite way!'
** How's that, umpire?

Classroom, where there's no disrespect!

EARWORM
[*EER-wurm*]

You walk past a busker,
a girl playing guitar for
coins. You stop to listen.

   She sings about little green
apples in the summertime,
making your toes tap. You
don't sing along, that would
be odd. Instead you smile and
dig in your pockets for any loose change.
Or you badger your mum for her loose change.

   Later, long after you've turned the corner, the girl
is gone but the tune lingers in your head, those
summertime apples so green and catchy – and you
can't get rid of the melody, no matter how hard you try.

   Bad luck. You have an **EARWORM** for company.
Try all you like, sing a different song, say the alphabet
backwards – the song is stuck, those apples there to
stay. Worse than apples, there's a worm inside the
music, the girl's tune becoming a bug in your brain.

 Other possible earworm cures are ten quick star-
jumps. Or chatting with a friend. Or you sing the
whole song from start to finish, if you can, shaking
the tune unstuck.

EDDY

[ED-ee]

Pull the plug and watch the magic happen.

In your kitchen sink, I mean. That **tiny whirlpool** twisting around the hole, just before the water vanishes with a *glurk*.

Massive whirlpools swallow ships. But an **EDDY** is fun for everyone, those mini-whirlpools we see wheeling in basins and baths, turning like a liquid tornado. You can make an eddy by churning your hand in the sea, carving a funnel on the surface.

Vikings gave us *ida*, their word for **whirlpool,** which English slowly spun into eddy. When you pull an oar, the blade leaves a wake of eddies behind the boat. Hey, maybe that's how you can tell the difference. Oar = eddy. Awe = whirlpool.

 Q: How do you know if a fish has been in your bathroom?

A: Because of the scales on the floor.

EPHEMERAL

[ih-FEM-er-uhl]

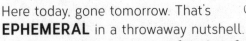

Here today, gone tomorrow. That's **EPHEMERAL** in a throwaway nutshell.

Flowers that bloom for **a few brief days** are called ephemeral. Butterflies are ephemeral too, a dainty flutter of wings doomed to die before the week is done.

Crazes are crazes because they're ephemeral – cool one day, cold the next. Name any fad, from Pokémon Go to fidget spinners, and you will see how fads are as fleeting as butterflies.

And if you keep a scrapbook then you might hang on to tickets or stickers as random souvenirs of your life. Bookmarks and boarding passes are called **ephemera** (with no l) because they usually go in the rubbish – unless you trap them in a scrapbook.

Ephemeral comes from *hemera*, the Greek word for **day**, the ticking clock of life and death already loaded into the letters.

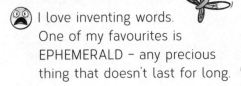

I love inventing words. One of my favourites is EPHEMERALD – any precious thing that doesn't last for long.

FARNARKLE
[far-NAR-kuhl]

John Clarke grew up in New Zealand, where he loved playing sport. Rugby and cricket and pool – the table game with balls, not the wet thing you jump into.

But one sport he never played was **farnarkling**. Can you guess why? Because John made it up.

Farnarkling was a nonsense game where players had to **arkle** the **fluker** around the **sward's grommet**. See, it makes no sense. The words were pure baloney, the whole sport created by John as a joke, his way of poking fun at how people talk so seriously about sport.

Every week, on Australian TV, John would have a chuckle at lots of things, from big politicians to big business. His way of telling jokes was to act as if the nonsense was real. We call this **satire**, a shrewd way of showing the audience just how stupid real things can be.

Imagine a game that nobody ever saw or understood, but with match reports every week. That was farnarkling. The satire was so fabulous that people used **FARNARKLE** to mean being busy, but really doing nothing at all.

John died while birdwatching in 2017, but even now he lives in our memory as well as the dictionary, all thanks to his fine farnarkling.

 Q: What sport do people play in dreams?

A: Bedminton

FLIBBERTIGIBBET

[*FLIB-er-tee-JIB-it*]

Some words in English are bliss to say, and one of those is **FLIBBERTIGIBBET**. Sounds like a frog playing jazz, doesn't it? Turns out the truth is just as dizzy, just as surprising.

Any kid who likes to **chatter** and **buzz about** is a flibbertigibbet, a born pest like the flies that frogs love to eat.

When my younger sister, Lib, was even younger, the family called her a flibbertigibbet – a cross between a **nuisance** and a **chatterbox**. Don't get me wrong: we all loved Lib. We still do. But she was a manic ball of energy, a flurry of fiddle-power. In a bonus way, LIB deserved her label, thanks to her name nestling in the letters of FLIBBERTIGIBBET.

Nobody knows how flibbertigibbet came to be. Maybe the word mocks the burble of small talk, that singsong rhythm of voices at a party. Or perhaps a noisy-nosy pain of a child reminds people of a frog with a trumpet.

Flibbertigibbet was first seen in 1549, in Middle English books – proof that humans have loved to chitchat for almost 500 years.

If LIB is a FLIBBERTIGIBBET (sorry, Lib), then what girl might you call AMIABLE? Or EXTRAVAGANT? Or EXHILARATING? Or WANDERING? If you don't know, look inside each word.

Mia, Ava, Lara, Erin

FRUNK

[FRUNK]

Elon Musk is an **imagineer** – an engineer who relies on his imagination. Born in South Africa, living in America, Musk is the man who longs to fly to Mars to start a village up there, just east of Venus.

Musk is also the man behind Tesla cars, those electric models humming along our roads. Each Tesla, unlike other models on the freeway, has a **FRUNK** to store the luggage.

The Volkswagen Beetle also has a frunk, a luggage space up-front, but the word didn't exist fifty years ago, when Beetles were more common.

Frunk blends two words: **front** plus **trunk**. Yet here in Australia we call a trunk a **boot**, possibly making the Tesla hatch a **froot**, a radical space to hold your bananas.

Standard cars hide their engines in their noses. But Mr Musk and the Tesla team prefer to pack a battery down the back, lending extra boost from behind. That way the front pocket is kept spare for suitcases.

A friend of mine says Elon's name is not really Elon, but a mixed-up way of writing Noel. He thinks Elon sounds more like the future, exactly the sort of name that creates labs on Mars or designs a frunk – or a froot.

😐 Nikola Tesla was also an imagineer, a Serbian-American who learnt the secrets of electricity one hundred years ago. Can you find TESLA hiding across two words on this page?

'Creates labs'.

FURPHY
[FUR-fee]

'Do you know Mr Murphy? He teaches piano at the school. Anyhow, I saw him last weekend with Ms Kamiakis, the principal. At the shops. Holding hands. They must be lovers.'

We hear rumours all the time, juicy bits of news people love to spread – even if nobody can prove them. No matter. The hearsay keeps coming. We hear about movie stars and teachers, sporting heroes and even our own friends.

The playground is popular for rumour-sharing, a patch of shade the perfect stage for the *Daily Gossip Show*. But a hundred years ago, a lot more people met on the battleground. Over in France, during World War I, soldiers crammed into trenches or waited in paddocks to fill their flasks. Fill their brains too, with fresh stories.

John **FURPHY** was a blacksmith during wartime. Stoking his furnace in country Victoria, Mr Furphy made steel tanks for the army – the kind of tanks for filling, not killing. Furphy's water tanks were massive barrels on wheels. Soon the whole thing was nicknamed a furphy. And a little later, a furphy was any **bogus** story, a false **rumour** swapped by soldiers waiting to get their daily fill.

 Q: What do you send a farmer with no water on his farm?

A: A Get Well Soon card

FURTIVE
[FUR-tiv]

Fox-like people are **FURTIVE**. They do things when nobody is watching. A furtive glance is a **sly** check. A furtive smile is a **secret** smirk, usually aimed at someone else who shares that secret with the smirker.

Furtive links to **fur**, though not the foxy type of fur. The real root is **thief**, or *fur* in old Rome, quite different from mink coats and foxtails. In fact, furtive thieves may steal furs.

Speaking of furs, a furtive person can also be described as **cloak-and-dagger**, since they may be hiding a knife in their pocket, a lethal weapon tucked out of sight.

Then there's the ferret, that weird rabbit-hunter who's shaped like a fox. **Ferret** also comes from *fur*, the old Latin thief, but I don't recommend you walk the street in ferret fur. Or any fur for that matter. Fur is seen as a cruel costume in this modern age, unless you favour faux-fur. Or you prefer to wear real fur furtively.

FURTIVE has FIVE on the outside. Can you fill these dashes to make more words?

O _ _ NE   F _ _ OUR

S _ _ _ IX   E _ _ _ IGHT

N _ _ _ _ _ INE   TE _ _ _ _ N

GLABELLA

[*gluh–BEL-uh*]

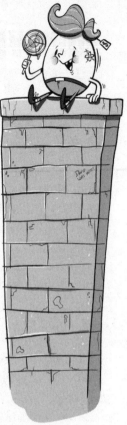

Jack's got one. Jill's got one. Even Miss Muffet's got one. Though I'm not sure about Humpty Dumpty.

You have one too, bang between your eyebrows. Put your finger there, just above your nose. Now trace the smooth skin stretching upward, ending at the lower edge of your forehead.

There, that's it – your **GLABELLA**, a sleek triangle of flat skin keeping your eyebrows apart.

The word comes from *glabellus*, the Latin word for **smooth**. Glabrous, in fact, is an old-fashioned word for **bald**. The movie star Dwayne Johnson, better known as The Rock, is glabrous as an actual rock.

As for Humpty Dumpty, if an egg has eyes but no eyebrows, can it own a glabella? Not a question you hear every day. To reach the right answer, you'll need to wrinkle your glabella from all the brain strain.

 Every answer ends in ELLA:

1. Rain shelter (8) **2.** Villain de Vil (7)
3. Midnight bolter? (10) **4.** Australian parrot (7)
5. Stretchy cheese (10) **6.** Kneecap (7)

1 umbrella, 2 Cruella, 3 Cinderella, 4 rosella, 5 mozzarella, 6 patella

GNOMON
[NOH-mon]

Before computers, before phones, before vacuum cleaners, there was even a time without clocks. What a time to be alive – presuming anyone knew the time.

Near enough was good enough back then. Rather than meet a mate at 3:15 pm, you met them after lunch sometime, or when the rain stopped, or between fencing classes.

Fussier people relied on the sun, measuring shadows creeping over the ground. And if you wished to be even more precise, you built a **sundial**.

Old gardens in older cities have those. They resemble stone tables with a metal beak in the middle. The beak is the **GNOMON** – a shape throwing shadows over the surface. Exact shadows too, their dark edge touching the numbers carved into the dial, telling you when that rendezvous is due.

Gnomon is from the old Greek, where *gnosis* was the word for **knowledge**. That's because the gnomon's shadows knew the time, obeying the sun around the clock.

 Q: Why is your grandad just like a sundial?

A. Both are old timers.

GOBBLEDEGOOK

[*GOB-uhl-dee-guhk*]

Kimigayo wa chiyo ni yachiyo ni sazare-ishi...
   If you've reached this far, you must be patient. Patient and bamboozled, unless you happen to speak Japanese.

   Those first few lines belong to Japan's national anthem – wishing the emperor a long life – but for everyone else the words are **GOBBLEDEGOOK**.

   Or gobbledygook – you can spell it two ways. Take your pick. One way or the other, the word refers to a burst of blah-blah you can't understand.

   Japanese or nonsense, the effect is the same. Unless you come from Tokyo or speak **mumbo jumbo** – another word for gobbledegook.

   Gobbledegook the word was invented by a Texan lawyer. His name was Maury Maverick, a relation of the cowboy who gave us another weird word that's coming in thirty pages or so. A big grab-bag of Gs and Bs, gobbledegook sounds like a panicky turkey, the ideal label for any message that makes you 😵.

 POPPYCOCK, another word for gobbledegook, doesn't relate to poppy flowers or noisy roosters. No, the word tells a Dutch story, coming from *pappekak*, or soft cow-poo!

GOOGLEGANGER
[*GOO-guhl-GANG-uh*]

One dark night, David Astle drove into a moose. The accident was messy and eerie all wrapped into one, mostly because David Astle (me) has never seen a moose in the wild. Not on a road. Not in the forest. Nowhere except on TV, really.

To explain things, the moose-man Astle is not the word-man Astle, better known as me. Nor am I to be confused with a sea captain called David Astle, or the David Astle who spent a night in jail for being unruly at a soccer match.

Tap your own name into Google and you'll find an army of yous across the world. Have you already done it? Scanning the net for your name is called **ego-surfing**, and only liars say they've never done it.

I did it. That's how I found each **GOOGLEGANGER**, another word for **namesake**, anyone who shares your name online. *Ganger* is a German word for **goer**, one who walks beside you, a **companion**.

Before the web, David Astle the London plumber probably never knew about David Astle the ostrich farmer in Perth. But now they do, thanks to search engines.

 Before Google was Google, the search engine was going to be called Backrub. Don't believe me? Look it up.

GROAK

[*GROKE*]

Frogs go croak, while dogs go **GROAK**. Not the noise, but their annoying dinnertime habit of staring at your food with **hungry eyes**.

Labradors are the worst, or the best, depending how you measure groaking. Even the most obedient dog has trouble aiming their gaze away from your spaghetti.

Cats groak too. Try opening a tin of tuna and see if your puss can resist groaking at your feet, meowing as they **stare**.

Groak can also be a noun, meaning your corgi or pesky brother could be groaks, or be the rascals responsible for a few desperate groaks as you try to dine. The word is Scottish, also appearing as growk, grook, grouk, groke or groach. That's a lot of different ways to say 'Please stop staring at me and go away!'

Croak and groak are not the only English words ending in OAK. Name two more. (And then name two words ending in ELM, another tree.)

Cloak, soak; helm, overwhelm

HABOOB

[huh-BOOB]

HABOOB is not a word you want to encounter in the desert.

Nomads known as Bedouins, people who roam the scalp of Africa, created the word. Crossing the Sahara for a living, the Bedouins know how nasty the desert can turn.

A puff of wind is fine. A gust, you can still cope. But when a haboob hits the dunes, a gale laced with sand, you need to take cover.

The word comes from Arabic, the language of the Bedouins. It means **blowing furiously**, just like haboobs do, sending bits of grit into every camel nostril, every unshut mouth, every fold of cloth.

Here in Australia, we might meet haboobs on the beach, but we usually call them **squalls** or **southerly busters**. Never pretty. And just as gritty.

 Q: What do you call a camel with a flat back?

HAYWIRE

[*HAY-wihr*]

If a computer goes **HAYWIRE**, the program crashes, the mouse misfires, your screen blinks and every byte is toothless. If plans go haywire, they go **out of control**.

Yet away from plans and computers, haywire is also tie-wire for hay, the metal band that binds a bale of cattle fodder. So how do the two haywire meanings connect? Can you link the wire-wire with the wacky-wire?

Ask any farmer. They'll know. One careless snip of a bundled bale and the wire will whip the air like a cranky snake.

That's one possible link, how wildly the wire recoils. The other link is how some farmers use the wire to mend machines, bending it in windmill motors or tractor engines instead of buying proper parts. Fix the motor right, and you save money. Fix it wrong, and the tractor might plough down your barn, going haywire.

 Q: What did the farmer call the cow that gave no milk?

A: An udder failure.

HOBNOB

[*HOB-nob*]

Hob is a stove that needs firewood to work. Hob is also a pixie, like those hobgoblins who haunt the fairytales.

Nob is slang for head, or a two-headed coin that cheats use to win a toss. A fussy snob is also a nob, and so too a rounded hill.

HOBNOB, on the other hand, has nothing to do with elves or stoves or heads or hills. Anyone who can hobnob can mingle well at parties, saying hello to every guest, no matter if those people are dear friends or dreary snobs.

William Shakespeare, the famous writer, first used hobnob in his plays, a catchy word meaning **to drink together**.

Drinking in fact is how hob and nob came to sit together. Hob comes from *habbe*, Old English for **have**. While nob comes from *nabbe*, Old English for **not-have**.

Can you guess why two opposites are friends? Picture two people drinking together. First one person has a glass in the air (making a toast to friendship), and then the other hobnobber takes their turn, drinking and refilling their cups as they go.

 To hobnob willy-nilly at a picnic you need to join the hubbub of chitchat.

HUMBLEBRAG

[*HUM-buhl-BRAG*]

Say you catch a wave. The wave is huge but you keep your cool, your balance, reaching the end of the wave's face at supersonic speed.

If you're **humble**, you paddle back for another ride, quiet and calm. If you're the opposite, you **brag**. Bragging means bellowing about yourself or your wave or your board, or anything unbearable for others to hear.

HUMBLEBRAG is a rare sandwich, much like hobnob, two opposites joining forces, a quiet-talker next-door to a bigmouth.

Humblebraggers show off slyly. That's the secret. Obvious boasters declare how cool they are, how smart, how rich, but not the humblebragger. Instead, they sprinkle facts that make them look good. Now and then they make remarks that don't make much noise but always whisper how wonderful they are. How kind. How amazing.

If I wasn't such a brilliant writer, I'd tell you how to do it.

 Q: Why don't surfers say hello?

ILLEISM

[*ILL-ee-izz-uhm*]

Way back when you were a toddler, you fell over in the park. Remember? Your knee was bleeding, not too much, but enough to start the waterworks, and the wailing. Your mum got up from the bench to say: 'Come here, darling, let Mummy kiss it better.'

Or your dad did the same thing, putting his phone down, and going, 'Hey, tiger, Dad will give you a hug.'

Both your parents are guilty of **ILLEISM**, where Mum or Dad or Elmo don't say 'I', but 'Mum', 'Dad' or 'Elmo'. A bit like Santa asking, 'What can Santa give you this year?'

Illeism comes from *ille* in Latin, which means **he**. Man or woman, Santa or Elmo, more people do it, using their names instead of saying me or I. 'Maddie is a big fan of hiphop,' says Maddie. 'Don't annoy Adam when he's hungry,' warns Adam.

Nothing to do with illness, illeism is a modern sickness, David believes.

 As more people share their lives (and dog photos) on Facebook and Instagram, illeism is growing, casting people as the main character in their own story.

INTERROBANG
[*in-TER-uh-bang*]

You and your friends are telling spooky stories around a campfire, eager to scare each other, trying to make your blood run cold. One friend, let's call her Sasha, says, 'Is that a ghost I can see?'

Maybe she asked quietly, almost in a murmur. But chances are she went, 'Is that a ghost I can see!'

Write it that way, with an exclamation mark, and you get the volume of Sasha's shout. But where did the question mark go? Somehow that vanished into thin air.

Enter the **INTERROBANG**, an inky swirl mingling a question mark with an exclamation mark, just the thing for any shouty-question or nosy-shout. Invented by a man named Martin Speckter about 50 years ago, the interrobang looks like this: **‽**

Interrobang is a blend of **interrogate** (to ask a question) and **bang**, old printing slang for an exclamation mark.

As for Sasha, that wasn't a ghost she saw but rather a nearby camper, telling you kids to stop scaring everybody and go to bed. But Sasha refused. She argued back. Typical Sasha. I mean, Sasha is *sooo* annoying. Seriously, who needs a friend like Sasha‽

Is that a ghost I can hear‽ (What word or name on this page sounds like another for ghost?

Speckter (spectre)

ISABELLINE

[izz-uh-BELL-een]

Are you called Izzy? Then get your mum to pop a bottle of fake champagne, because your name is a word in the dictionary.

ISABELLINE is **yellowy brown**, like the colour of real champagne or an old pony. The word honours a Spanish princess born four hundred and fifty years ago. Her full name was Isabella Clara Eugenia, but everyone called her Izzy.

She married her cousin Albert VII, the sequel to Albert VI. Together they ruled a big chunk of Europe, except for one city in Belgium called Ostend. Everyone in Ostend said, 'We don't want to be ruled by two creepy cousins.'

So the royal army encircled the city, waiting for Ostenders to surrender. Isabella was confident her husband would win the Big Wait Contest, which soldiers call a **siege**. So sure, she promised to wear the same undies until Ostend waved the white flag.

She waited. And waited. For three 'hole' years, never changing her mind or her undies. And that's the legend of isabelline, the colour of grotty knickers worn, and worn, and worn by a stubborn princess.

In the end, Ostend fell to Spain, while Princess Isabella almost fell to her smell.

 Isabella was the most popular baby girl's name in 2009, beating Chloe and Charlotte despite the smelly knickers story.

JACUZZI

[*juh-KOOZ-ee*]

Maybe you know the **tub**, but do you know the tale behind the tub?

JACUZZI is another word for **spa**, the kind you find beside pools, or inside gyms and modern homes. Despite r (the letter) skipping jacuzzi (the word), the tub is devoted to aah (the sigh).

Jacuzzi began as a brand, linked to a family of inventors, a big American clan who originally came from Italy. Giocondo Jacuzzi was the first to show his talents, designing propellers in the early 1920s. Alas, young Giocondo died in a plane crash soon after.

But the Jacuzzis stayed strong. They persevered, making propellers and pumps, until baby Kenneth came along in 1941. Early in his life, little Kenneth's body was racked with aches and pains, his torment inspiring a different line of inventions.

Why not build a whirlpool tub to soothe the soaker's body? That was the new plan. The bath's currents worked miracles on young Kenneth, a natural massage to make his limbs more flexible. Countless bubbles eased his aches. Overnight the Jacuzzis went from producing planes to reducing pains, their brand-new jets made of water.

 Sometimes two words, what other invention made for watery pleasure also starts with J and ends with I?

Jetski

JETTISON
[*JET-uh-suhn*]

Do you have a favourite reality show? The best/worst part is how each episode ends, when someone has to go home.

It's tough. You follow the singers so closely, the cooks, the bachelors, whoever you follow – only for the judges to say goodbye. Pack your bags. Go on, get!

Cruel, but those are the rules. Every show, the jury must **JETTISON** a contestant, just like a balloonist jettisons a sandbag to make his basket lighter, or a boss jettisons workers to make her staff smaller.

Jettison means to **throw off**, to **throw away**. Your dad might jettison holey socks just as your mum might jettison the muddy dog off the couch.

Jettison comes from *jactare* in Latin, the old word for **throw.** So many words belong to the *jactare* family, like **eject** (to throw out), or **jetsam** (the cargo that captains throw overboard), or even **jeté**, the ballet jump.

Jet is another cousin. If you can't guess why, just buckle into a 747 and wait for the engines to throw you back into your seat.

 Q: What sound does a 747 make when it makes a rough landing?

A: Boeing, Boeing, Boeing

50

JUFFLE
[*JUFF-fuhl*]

Do you **JUFFLE**?

A common place for juffling is a zebra crossing when cars are waiting for you to cross. Since you're a thoughtful human being, you might quicken your step a little, just to lessen the drivers' delay.

Juffling is a mix of **jogging** and **shuffling**, a semi-scoot with an extra shimmy, though it's not really that quick. More a show of speed than a genuine hurry, juffling is an effort to move *fastish*, instead of fast, yet never so fastish you pull a muscle or get your hair out of place.

After all, cars at zebra crossings have to wait for you to cross. On the other hand, friends on the move, if they are real friends, will slow down until you juffle up level.

Truth is, we already know that, which is why we juffle. This strange non-speed is our silent way of saying, 'Even though I don't need to hurry, look, I'm a nice person.'

What word meaning **to walk slowly** can be jumbled to spell a word meaning **to walk like a duck**?

Dawdle, waddle

JUGGERNAUT

[*jug-gah-NORT*]

Watch out! There's a truck full of watermelons speeding downhill!

Even if you love watermelons, run. Fast. There's no time for juffling when you're faced with the scary power of a **JUGGERNAUT** – a large, uncontrollable force, with or without watermelons.

The word comes from India, naming a **massive chariot** made to carry a Hindu god statue. The god was called Jagannath, meaning **Lord of the Universe** in Hindi.

At certain times in the calendar, the chariot was towed through towns – not by horses, but by the people who worshipped Jagannath. Soon the god and the giant cart became the one word.

So deep was the people's belief, they'd erupt into a frenzy, yelling and bellowing, or even diving beneath the chariot's wheels, only to be crushed like watermelons.

Not that juggernauts need wheels to be juggernauts. Say you insist your sister is a zombie. And say that lie spreads across the school, making everyone think your sister eats brains for breakfast. Well, you just started a juggernaut, a force that can't be stopped.

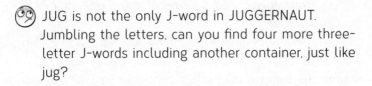 JUG is not the only J-word in JUGGERNAUT. Jumbling the letters, can you find four more three-letter J-words including another container, just like jug?

KALAMAZOO

[KAL-a-mah-ZOO]

Know a **KALAMAZOO** or two? If you live by a railway, there's a reasonable chance, even though kalamazoos are rare as hen's teeth.

Back in the 1800s, these funky carts were more common, a mini-train built for two. The name comes from Kalamazoo, an American town famous for making stoves and windmills, mandolins and paper plates – plus funky little railroad carts.

Rich people loved to rocket around in their private kalamazoos, powered by pedals, or a seesaw gadget, or even slaves running at the back. But too many kalamazoos spoiled the fun for everyone, blocking real trains trying to do their train thing.

Some people know kalamazoos as **handcars**, which is a bit boring. **Pump trolley** is a neater nickname, and funnier – just like **jigger**, another label. In Germany the kalamazoo is called *Laufmaschiner* – or running machine.

The man to imagine the running machine, was Baron Karl Drais. Never barren for ideas, the baron also invented a typewriter, a meat grinder, a bicycle and a wood-fired stove. But the for all his flair, the German never invented a name as nifty as kalamazoo.

 Q: What's the difference between a rail conductor and a teacher?

A: One minds the train, while the other trains the mind.

KIRIGAMI

[*kir-i-GAH-mee*]

Rock/paper/scissors – which do you choose?

If you chose rock, bad luck. You have no role to play in our next story. But scissors, on the other hand (or in the other hand), are just as important as paper.

At least when it comes to **KIRIGAMI**, a craft a bit like origami: folding paper into shapes, but this time with scissors allowed.

Sliced in half, KIRIGAMI makes two Japanese words to mean **cut** + **paper**. (Well, actually *kami* means paper in Japanese, but *kirikami* is slightly harder to say. Slightly.)

And if that feels like cheating, changing Japanese sounds to fit English mouths, then what about flashing knives and scissors to make a paper castle?

Origami lovers are wary of kirigami, thinking snipping is taking short-cuts, but the hobby has blossomed in the last hundred years, the creasing craze slowly increasing. Put together, paper and scissors rock!

😉 **Q:** Did you hear about the origami school with no students?

A: It was forced to fold.

55

KOWTOW

[*KOU-TOU*]

Knock, knock.
  Who's there?
  Cow.
  Cow who?
  KOWTOW.
  Cow what? **KOWTOW**, I said – a word meaning **knock-head** in Chinese. The best way to explain this word is to apologise...

  Due to that joke, and its lame punchline, I'm desperate for you to forgive me. Can we still be friends? Please, please, don't make me beg.

  Okay, if you must, I will kowtow to you, getting down on my knees and knocking my forehead on the floor. That's how kowtowing works, where a prisoner may beg for mercy, or a worker may seek kindness from a tyrant.

  So, did my humble head-knocking work? Do you want to hear some more knock-knock jokes? Cross my heart, these are better.

 Knock, knock. Who's there? Cash. Cash who?
  No thanks, I have a nut allergy.

  Knock, knock. Who's there? Spell. Spell who?
  W-H-O.

  Knock, knock. Who's there? Deja. Deja who?
  Knock, knock...(Mum or Dad will tell you why that joke is dynamite.)

KVETCH
[kfech]

As a kid, one of my favourite toys was the **Etch-A-Sketch**. The French called them **magic screens** because that's how they seem.

A flat box with a red frame, the toy has a silver screen and a knob in either corner you need to twist and turn. Twiddle them well, and you draw a picture on the screen, like drawing in sand with an invisible stick.

The reason I'm telling you all this is due to the robbery. One day my brother stole my Etch-A-Sketch. Sorry. My brother *borrowed* it without telling me. Do your toys get stolen like this? Not by Richard, my brother, but by people in your own family?

When I saw my magic screen was missing I went to tell Mum. She laughed and said, 'Stop being an Etch-A-Sketch **KVETCH**.'

Kvetch is a Yiddish word, from the wonderful Jewish language. It means **to complain**, or someone who loves to complain. So what happened to my toy, you ask? Well, after a stretch, this wretch of an Etch-A-Sketch kvetch had to go fetch.

 Q: Where do sour grapes grow?

LACKADAISICAL
[lak-uh-DAY-zee-kuhl]

Once upon a time, when a person didn't want to get out of bed, they took a deep breath and sighed, 'O lackaday...'

Notice how **Oh** was **O** back then. And also notice how **lackaday** doesn't make any sense. Not to a reader in this millennium. But lackaday was a dramatic way of saying **poor, poor me** – a shorter way of saying **alas the day**. In other words, 'What a terrible day I'm having. Life feels such a chore.'

'I feel so foul I dare not leave this bed,' sayeth this old lazybones. And when a person persists in being so lazy and repeating lackaday every hour, they're labelled **LACKADAISICAL**.

Nowadays we say **slack**. Or **idle**. Or even **careless**, if the person is so lazy they don't concentrate on what they're doing. 'Stop being so lackadaisical!' you might hear a parent yell in a supermarket, though slack is quicker to yell if the parent is feeling lazy.

 Q: What do you call a lackadaisical pop star?

A: A teen idle.

LAMBENT

[*LAM-buhnt*]

LAMBENT has nothing to do with bending lambs into hamburgers or rolling them into wraps.

Let's think about cakes instead. When's your next birthday? Mine's in November, but I'm too old for the usual fuss. Besides, with so many candles on my cake, the flames might scorch the ceiling.

But when your turn comes, and the candles get lit, then watch the flames dance for a while. See how they wobble, swaying their bright hips in the breeze.

Lambent is the word for this moment, another way of saying **bright** or **flowing**. It comes from *lambere* in Latin, meaning **to lick**, just as poets describe how bonfires lick the sky. Someone with dazzling eyes can also have a lambent gaze. It's a very romantic word.

But let's not get distracted. You have a job to do. Take a breath, make a wish and blow out those lambent candles.

 Q: Why can't you trust a candle?

A: Because they're wicked

LAVA-LAVA

[lah-vuh-LAH-vuh]

What do you wear when you go from the shower to your bedroom? Do you streak in the nude or dash in your undies?

Or Option 3 – do you wrap a towel around your hips?

If you do, that towel could be a **LAVA-LAVA**, a word we borrow from Samoa in the Pacific. Long ago a lava-lava was made from palm leaves, but lately fabric is more the island fad, a single sheet hanging from hips to shins.

Should the lava-lava be shorter, the **skirt** turns into a **lap-lap** – a popular garment in Papua New Guinea.

Then again, if your lava-lava is extra long, stretching from your shoulders to your ankles, you may be wearing a **muu-muu**. Not a cow but a single-cloth dress that's cool in Hawaii because Hawaii can get hot.

Can you jumble GROANS to make another Pacific wrap-dress, one that hangs from hips to ankles?

Sarong, a word from the Malay language

LEVIDROME
[LAIRV-ee-drome]

Kayak can paddle in either direction, making the same word each time. Right to left, left to right, kayak is always kayak. We call this a **palindrome**.

Peek does a different trick, becoming **keep** on the rebound. **Sleep** makes **peels** in reverse. If a boy from Canada gets his wish, we'd call this sort of word a **LEVIDROME**, where **spot** make **tops** when spinning.

Levi Budd loves how **Levi** can be jumbled into **live**, and **live** can switch into **evil**, which makes it another levidrome, a word he invented when he was six. His dad – a history writer named Lucky – shared Levi's levidrome on Facebook, and lots of people went **wow**, which is a palindrome, just like **dad**.

Several dictionaries use the word **emordnilap** to describe these **dog-god** doubles. As you can tell, emordnilap is palindrome backwards. But emordnilap is tough to say, so Levi wants to live to see levidrome get the don. I mean, the nod.

For that to happen, people like **Liam (mail)**, **Mia (aim)** and all their **pals (slap)** need to use levidrome, plus hundreds of other kids. What word will you invent for the dictionary?

There are five common levidrome animals. BAT is one – making TAB when flying back. Can you nab the other four?

Rat, dog, deer, wolf. Find any others?

MACGUFFIN
[*mack-GUFF-in*]

Thriller movies thrill, as people dodge bullets or dive out of helicopters. But all this action has to have a why – a reason for the risk-taking. Every spy in the story, every baddie and hero, needs a prize to chase.

Perhaps an Aztec vase needs saving, or a bag of money must be found. Or maybe there's a **MACGUFFIN** up for grabs.

Alfred Hitchcock, an English film director, coined the word to mean a mystery object lying at the heart of a mystery story.

It can be anything – a trophy, a hostage, a rare football card. So long as every character is desperate to save it, or own it, that's all that counts – even if nobody truly understands what it is.

Or they might understand, all those chasers on the big screen, but we in the audience don't get it. Nor do we care, so long as the chasing stays exciting, the stunts and fights keep coming – the MacGuffin can find itself.

Obviously if a hostage is in danger, we care. But with half the action movies, the reward is hazy, and only gets hazier as each scene rolls by. Sometimes MacGuffin feels like Hollywood slang for nuffin!

 Q: Where does a mermaid like to watch movies?

A: At the dive-in

MANTICORE

[*MAN-tic-aw*]

A dragon is big and scaly and breathes fire, and that's that. Nothing more to it.

Compare that to the **MANTICORE**, a **monster** with a lion's body, a scorpion's tail and a man's head with three rows of teeth.

In other storybooks, the manticore's tail is more like a spike that shoots arrows. Those teeth can also be arranged in two or four rows, depending which legends you gobble.

As if that's not enough, some legends insist the manticore owns a tiger's torso, monkey's paws, plus an old man's head with bonus horns and tusks. Make up your minds, myth-makers!

Manticore the name comes from Persia, an ancient land that had its share of monsters. The original name was *mardkhora*, or **man-eater**. So let's agree on something – if you see a beast with tusks and spikes and stripes and horns, it's dinnertime, and you're it.

Another scary beast from Persian folklore is the ROC, a mammoth bird with skull-crushing claws. Now look backwards in MANTICORE and there's the roc nesting!

MAVERICK

[*MAV-uh-RICK*]

Samuel **MAVERICK** ran a ranch in Texas with plenty of cows. How many cows, we'll never know. That's because Sam had a funny way of ranch-running.

To explain, every other cow-owner in Texas had a brand. Unlike Nike, or Vegemite, each brand was a metal design the farmer would burn into his cattle's hide. It's why we say brand today, to mean a logo belonging to a company.

But Mr Maverick had no brand. Instead he said any calf found roaming Texas without a brand was his. A clever plan, when you think about it. Because if any cowboy forgot to burn his mark on his herd, then Samuel Maverick could steer another owner's steer to his place.

Miles from ranches, a maverick is anyone who ignores the usual way of doing things. If you ran a cross-country race from the finish to the start, you'd be a maverick. And disqualified. Because being a maverick is rarely easy – but think of all the rewards you might gain, not to mention the cows.

 Q: Why did the bow-legged cowboy get fired?

A: Because he couldn't keep his calves together.

MEGALOMANIAC

[*meg-uh-loh-MAY-nee-ak*]

Power is like a jumbo serve of chicken nuggets. One small taste of salt and spice, and you want the entire bucket.

Everything.

Maybe you know a teacher who's itching to run the whole school. Or Aunt Fiona tries to control every family get-together like she's a puppet master. Or imagine a zookeeper who thinks he's in charge of every animal inside and outside his zoo – the Supreme Boss of Beasts.

Each person would be a **MEGALOMANIAC**, a **sucker for power**, a mega-sized ego who longs to be *numero uno*.

Mega is another word for **huge**. **Maniac**, the second part, is a maniac, just like it says. Added up, a megalomaniac is a craver for bigness, a person hungry for outright control.

Do you know anyone like that? Please don't tell me it's you.

Can you scramble BOSSES to spell a word meaning **to drive crazy**? Every letter is used once only.

obsess

NARCISSIST

[NAHR-suh-sist]

Shop windows can act as mirrors. If the light is right, or the glass is tinted, you can see your own reflection looking back.

Numerous people take furtive peeks as they pass, checking their appearance on the move. Heading for the office, walking past a bank of windows, many workers glance in the glass to ensure they don't have cockatoo hair, like I get most mornings.

Nothing wrong with glancing. Ten times better than staring at your reflection all day, so close you can kiss your own mirror-lips.

That's how Narcissus behaved, his shop window a forest pool. The Greek boy could barely break his stare, admiring his reflection every minute of the day. Even Echo, his sweetheart, failed to undo the selfie spell. Her boy was lost. In his own image.

Thanks to this tale, written by a Roman poet called Ovid, we now call any big-time **self-lover** a **NARCISSIST**. Male or female – if someone only has eyes for the way they look or act, they're a narcissist, a me-me creature with eyes devoted to their own I.

There's a sad end to the story. Giddy with love, the boy reached for the water to hug himself and *ker-splosh*. Narcissus fell head over heels for real this time, drowning in his own deep mirror.

 Q: Did you hear about the narcissistic gnome?

A: He loved taking elfies

NEF

[*NEFF*]

NEF is not a word you really need. But if nobody needs it, then nef might die.

So next time you see a tiny ship sitting on a dinner table, an exquisite ornament with golden masts or pearls for portholes, make sure to say, 'My, what a nice nef.'

Since a nef is precisely that – a table-piece shaped like a ship. The word comes from *navis*, a Latin **ship**. French jewellers added the f, making their tiny model close to **naff**, which is British slang for **stupid**.

Which a nef isn't. It's elegant. Graceful. Rarer than rare. With wire cables and golden hull, a nef is dainty as well as handy, often carrying salt and pepper shakers like cargo, all in easy reach for diners.

So now you know a nef, you'll neffer forget.

What common seven-letter English word has NEF moored in the middle? Here's the pattern for you:

_ _ N E F _ _

Benefit, as well as tuneful

OCHE
[OCK-ee]

If you've thrown darts at a board, or Velcro balls at a fabric target, then you will know the secrets of the **OCHE**. Or your toes know, as they need to stay behind the oche, that mark on the floor where throwers have to stand.

If one little piggy goes over that oche, one centimetre of shoe leather, then the dart won't count. Your score is pointless.

Seems only fair, don't you think? Otherwise people could stand in reach of the target, sticking the darts into the bullseye like pressing tacks into a corkboard.

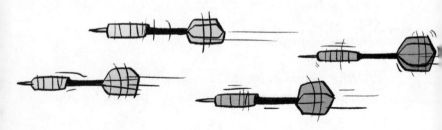

That's why you need an oche, which sounds like **hockey** without an **h**.

Oche comes from Old French, a language where *ocher* meant **to cut a notch**. Next time you throw darts or Velcro balls or coconuts, or maybe hula-hoops at the school fair, you'll need to play fair and plant your feet behind the oche, okay?

What four-letter word hides in OCHE? And can you make new words by mixing in an R? Or S? Or K? (And bullseye if you can toss P into OCHE to make a word!)

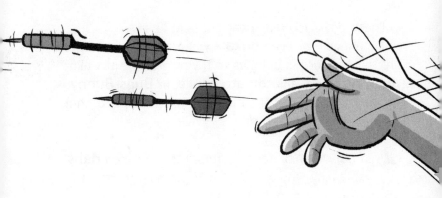

Echo; chore, ochre; chose; choke; epoch (a long stretch of time)

ONKAPARINGA

[ONK-ah-PARR-in-gah]

Grab a doona, grab a quilt. And if none of those is handy, grab an **ONKAPARINGA**, which is what some Aussies call a heavy blanket.

The word began as a brand, the Onkaparinga label stitched into the blanket's corner. **Doona** did the same trick, the bedcover company slipping into the dictionary as any normal word with a small **d**.

The Onkaparinga factory is named after the Onkaparinga River that flows south of Adelaide, in South Australia. If we keep pulling the threads, the Onkaparinga River is tied to the Kaurna people of that area, their own name being *ngangki-parri-ngka* – or 'on the women's river'.

These days, you may hear old people say onkaparinga – or even **onka** – when they mean **finger**. This bit of silliness belongs to rhyming slang, just like **dead horse** means **tomato sauce**, or **Bugs Bunny** is **money**. Maybe the sort of money you can spend on a factory-fresh onkaparinga.

 In old criminal slang, fingerprints are called **dabs**, explaining why burglars wear gloves – to stop their onkas leaving dabs behind.

OM

[*OM*]

OM is what Buddhist monks drone, far off in the mountains of Nepal or the bamboo groves of eastern Asia. Buddhism is based on the words of Siddhartha Gautama, a holy teacher from long ago, better known as Buddha, or the Awakened One.

Eyes shut, mind free, the monks utter om as a means of **meditation**, a sacred style of thinking, like running a deep bath for the brain. After years of practice, a serene monk can leave their day-to-day troubles behind.

Sitting in smoky temples or high on the brinks of cliffs, the holy men and women let their lungs do the talking, with just one word to utter. As much a breath as a word, the Buddhist om sounds like *ommmmmmmmm* – the more **ms** the better.

Om is a prayer of one syllable. What other word carries such inner peace? Try it. Close your eyes and om for a mo. Feel your body buzz, your body turning into an instrument. Hard to name another word that wields such wonder.

Of course, plenty of om jokes exist, keeping the **monk** in **monkeying around**. Meditate on these:

When monks are unsure, do they go ummmmm?

Do Buddhist electricians go ohmmmmm?

What do you call a monk's short trance? An omelette.

Laugh all you like, the devoted monks won't hear you, lost in the hum of their momentous oms.

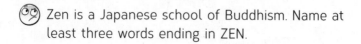 Zen is a Japanese school of Buddhism. Name at least three words ending in ZEN.

OMNISHAMBLES

[*OM-nee-SHAM-buls*]

Omni means **everything** in Latin – everything or everywhere. Pigs are **omnivores**, meaning they eat what they find, from beetles to lamingtons.

But two hundred years ago, when an English pig was fat from eating, it was led to market for humans to eat. Outside of London, the busiest square for fresh meat was in York. There, most of the butchers worked in The Shambles, a lane full of T-bones and chops, ribs and rumps.

Imagine the noise, the squeals and bleats, the red puddles on the stone floor. Soon Shambles the name became **shambles** the word, a jokey way of saying **one big mess**, a label for anywhere lacking peace or order.

Maybe your bedroom is a shambles – without the gore, I hope. Or your garage could be a similar pigsty, minus the bones and slabs of bacon.

As for **OMNISHAMBLES**, that's an **everything-mess**, the highest order of disorder. It's what a super-pig (or full-time slob) leaves behind. Forget the dustpan. You might need a firehose.

(◕◡◕) Time to rhyme each word below with another word for mess. If GAMBLES gives you SHAMBLES, or even OMNISHAMBLES, what other messes will emerge?

1. PUDDLE

2. BUTTER

3. BANGLE

4. ILLUSION

5. STUMBLE

6. BIG-PIE

7. FISH-CASH

8. DODGE-LODGE

OSCULATE

[OSS-kew-late]

'Oooooh, I saw you and your friend osculating the other day!'

Don't deny it. I know what I saw – your mum was osculating you, and some other mum was osculating your friend, both at the school gate. It was full-on!

OSCULATE is a quaint word for **kiss**. The word comes from Latin, where *osculum* means **a little mouth**, much like the osculum we make with our lips to smooch. *Mwah!*

Latin gives us loads of delicate words for simple actions. When you **stretch and yawn** at the same time, you are **pandiculating**. Bella, my Siberian cat, is a great pandiculator.

Meanwhile, to **pertussate** is to **cough**, while **masticate** means to **chew**. Next time, when your nose has a **sneeze** looming, make sure you say, 'Watch out, I'm going to **sternutate!**'

As for **flatulating**, that's sneezing at the other end of your body, if you get my drift – leaving a stink adrift in the air. Take care to translate which ate-word you mean before it's too late.

 Whenever a sneezer covers their mouth with the inside of their elbow, that's called a **vampire sneeze**, just like Dracula hiding his face in his cloak.

OUTLANDISH
[out-LAN-dish]

A strange word for **strange**, **OUTLANDISH** hints at distant mountains and remote valleys. The word murmurs a kingdom over the horizon. Think about it. If your homeland is what you know, then outlands are places you don't.

Wooden earrings from Borneo are outlandish in that way. A reindeer drum made by Inuit people is outlandish because Greenland is miles from your homeland.

Yet can you see the outlandish problem? Our planet is smaller now, thanks to jets and internet, satellites and Skype. The outlands of yesterday are now on TV. Why should lychees be outlandish just because they hail from China? I love lychees. Have you tried them with ice-cream? The fruit is delicious, not outlandish.

Far-fetched also means strange, just like outlandish. Any item fetched from distant corners of the earth – be it Borneo bling or Asian fruit – is likely to be unfamiliar. But if Google Earth puts the whole earth in reach, can outlandish remain outlandish?

 Q: If someone thinks the earth is flat, then how do they travel the world?

A: On a plane. (Maybe ask your teacher to explain that joke!)

PARAPH

[*PAR-uhf*]

When I was a kid my nickname was Astroboy. It makes sense when you know my surname, plus the way kids warp names into jokes or Japanese robots.

The nickname didn't last into high school. But just in case I was going to be Astroboy all my life, I spent long hours trying out my signature.

I scribbled on pads. On serviettes. In margins and exercise books. No matter the place, I liked to finish my signature with a squiggle. A wavy line or a cool swoosh, some kind of bold finale to underline my artwork.

The unusual name for that **squiggle** is a **PARAPH**, a close cousin of the block of text we call a **paragraph**. Both paraphs and paragraphs enclose letters, like fences enclose sheep. Maybe that's why sheep sleep in pens...

Napoleon Bonaparte, the French general, had a paraph longer than his name. Mozart the composer had a shallow spoon-swirl. If I asked you for your autograph, would you add your own paraph?

Pablo Picasso, the art genius, had a bold paraph to underline his autograph. (Can you jumble ART GENIUS to spell a word hiding on this page?)

Signature

PAREIDOLIA

[*pair-eye-DOH-lee-uh*]

You put the bread in the slot, push it down, wait a minute, then *pop* – your toast is ready.

But some people hesitate. They forget about the butter, the jam, and gawk at their toast on the plate. Somehow their slice has turned into a goldfish or a goblin or their Uncle Stuart.

Has that happened to you? If not Uncle Stuart, then have you seen someone else you recognise, a familiar face smiling from your toast, an eagle sketched by the cracks in a bathroom wall? Squirt sauce on your pie and you might see a politician in the puddle, depending how the splat spreads out.

This is **PAREIDOLIA**, a science term for seeing faces or pictures in **random shapes** and patterns.

Astronauts might think they see eyes and noses when they look at craters. Even on earth, looking up, we imagine a lunar face staring back. Just like a power point in the wall can resemble a person looking surprised.

Odd as it seems, everyone can get pareidolia. It's as normal as it is weird, seeing dinosaurs in paint splotches, a walrus smiling in your mayonnaise.

Pareidolia comes from Greek and means **wrong-image**. But if your toast bears a brilliant goldfish portrait, is that image wrong?

 In 2004, a ten-year-old called Diane Duyser saw Jesus on her cheese toastie. The Miami girl sold the sandwich on eBay for $28,000.

PERGOLA

[*purr-GOAL-ah... or PURR-gyu-lah*]

Mick is a carpenter who loves telling stories. One day, he told me, he went to a house that needed a **PERGOLA** in the garden.

Does your garden have one? Perhaps your park or school? Often made of wood, a pergola is a frame supported on posts, built for vines to twist around. Over time, as more plants grow, a pergola can turn into a green roof.

Ask some people, like my mate Mick, and they say pergola rhymes with **granola**. While other folks reckon the word sounds more like **burglar**, somehow the oh-sound being stolen.

(Which way do you say pergola? Dictionaries reckon both are fine, but that doesn't please Mick.)

It's why he pulled a face when the customer said she wanted a pergola, as in *PURR-gyu-lah* rather than Mick's version – *purr-GOAL-ah*.

Mick frowned. 'I'm sorry,' he said, putting his tape-measure away, jumping back in his truck. 'I don't know how to build a pergola, madam. I only know how to build a pergola.'

Jumble F into PERGOLA and you can spell what old-school jumping game? (The answer is a word for jump beside a well-known jumper!)

PETRICHOR
[PET-ree-kor]

The earth is parched, the paddocks are dust. There's been no rain for weeks. Then slowly the storm clouds gather. The sky turns bruised as all the dogs hide beneath the beds.

Thunder booms. The rain falls in sheets, like bedsheets of pure water. The best part? You stay dry under a tin roof, listening to the crazy drumming, the noise too loud for anyone to speak.

Afterwards, the road is aglow with puddles, all the gutters chuckling, the frogs in full song. Plus there's a powerful smell in the air, an electric perfume filling your nostrils.

Two Australian scientists, Isabel Bear and Richard Thomas, called this perfume **PETRICHOR**, the wonderful scent lacing the land after rain.

The aroma is a blend of plant oil and warming wet earth, the smell every Australian nose knows so well. Petrichor is a blend too. It joins two Greek words, where *petro* means **rock**, while *ichor* is the **holy fluid** flowing through the veins of gods.

Okay, dogs – it's safe to come out now.

What fuel, seabird, old-fashioned underwear, flower (and flower part) all start with PET?

Petrol, petrel, petticoat, petunia, petal

PLACEBO

[*plah-SEE-bo*]

Sometimes scientists can be crafty, seeking to make our world a safer place.

Imagine there's a new pill that makes the flu vanish in seven seconds. One minute you're sneezing and the next – *bingo* – you feel fine. Not a jot of snot to blurt on your shirt.

Of course everyone would swallow that pill. Let's call it FleeFlu. Yet before that pill can appear on the chemist shelf, the science labs need to check FleeFlu works.

To do that, they give the drug to fluey volunteers. Just to be careful, they also give a dummy FleeFlu to other sniffy types, telling them it's the *real* drug – and they swallow it. Both the fib and the fake FleeFlu.

The **dummy pill** is the **PLACEBO**, Latin for '**I shall please**'. The fake pill is to please the scientists, since they need to prove the genuine pill works – the drug and not the lolly masquerading as the drug. The best way to be sure is to see how the fluey folks fare with the fake FleeFlu – or placebo.

Doctor, doctor, I think I'm curtains! (Pull yourself together.)

Doctor, doctor, I think I'm a bridge! (What's come over you?)

Doctor, doctor, I think I'm a pack of cards! (I'll deal with you later.)

Doctor, doctor, I think I'm a dog! (Sit!)

Doctor, doctor, I think I'm a frog! (Don't croak.)

Doctor, doctor, I feel like a sheep. (That sounds baaaaad.)

Doctor, doctor, I think I'm shrinking. (Slow down. You just have to be a little patient.)

Doctor, doctor, I think I need glasses. (I agree. This is a bakery.)

Doctor, doctor, people keep ignoring me. (Next please.)

Doctor, doctor, I think I'm a vampire. (Necks please.)

PLIP

[*PLIP*]

Zoom. Splash. Whiz. Clunk.

Each word is a sound-word, echoing the noise the speaker can hear, from the sizzle of sausages to the rooster's cock-a-doodle-doo.

Onomatopoeia might sound like your dad gargling in the bathroom, but it's actually the proper name for a stick's snap, a fire's crackle, a balloon's pop.

Coming from Greek, onomatopoeia means **name-making**, since the balloon and rooster, and every other noise-maker, help to create their own sound-word.

But notice how most examples are old. Sticks and splashes have been around forever, along with a bell's bong, a spring's boing.

That's why I love **PLIP**, a new arrival in the onomatopoeia clan. One push of the electronic key and plip – your car unlocks. Or locks, depending on who's plipping what when and where.

 Rain in English goes pit-a-pat. But around the world, rain makes other noises, like *sou-sou* (Cantonese), *ju-ruk-ju-ruk* (Korean) or *csipp-csepp* (Hungarian).

PROPAGANDA

[prop-uh-GAN-duh]

PROPAGANDA sounds like **proper gander**, a total goose with feathers for brains, which suits the meaning of propaganda. Nothing to do with real birds, but more about fake news.

Let's say I told you aliens will land on Earth at 3 am tomorrow. Or maybe 3.30, as they may be running late. To persuade you, I have galaxy maps and videos of flying saucers.

Even more bizarre, these aliens will zap any kid who doesn't have a book in their hand. Unless you have a book as a shield, then *zorrfff*, you'll turn into a pyramid of green powder. So watch out!

Okay, that alien story is a lie. But more than a lie, it's propaganda – because publishers are paying me to spread this rumour, a sly trick to boost book sales. The lie has a plan behind it, urging you to act in a certain way by spreading **phony info** pretending to be true.

When farmers propagate wheat, they spread seed across the field. Same goes for propaganda, which spreads lies across town, across the internet, trying to plant a seed in your brain.

 Q: What do you call phony rigatoni?

PUMPERNICKEL

[*PUMP-ah-NICK-uhl*]

PUMPERNICKEL has no relation to pumps or nickel. And that's one reason I adore this word. Or two reasons. I can't decide.

Another reason is the taste. Pumpernickel is a **dark kind of bread**, made of rye and sour-tasting dough. Have you tried it? Thick and brown as cardboard, a slice is nice with salad or cheese or blobs of jam.

Pumpernickel is German, just like the bread. *Pumpern* in old German means **full of wind**, a polite way of saying **farty**, because a slice packs a smelly punch that way.

As for *nickel*, the word's second part, that points to **Nicholas**, an old-time label for the devil – his nickname in fact! That's why pumpernickel is a fiendish farter, a gassy demon, a hellish rogue who lets loose its smelly air for queen and country. One small plate and you're bound to detonate.

Poor old pumpernickel. The bread is unusual enough – dense as rubber, flat as a doormat. But imagine trying to sell yourself in a delicatessen as a smelly monster from the underworld.

PRUNE (another farty treat) hides inside PUMPERNICKEL. Keep sifting those letters and you'll also find a vegetable, plus another two fruits. Spin the letters if that helps, and see if you can find the missing fruit and veg.

Pumpkin, plum, lime

QUASI
[*KWAR-zee*]

QUASI seems half-finished. As if a spelling contestant had a brain fade, starting the word but then stopping, not quite sure how things were meant to end:

'Q-U-A-S-I...'

That fits quasi's meaning too, a word to describe something **not quite what it seems**. For example, if your teacher was sick one day, and you stood out the front, teaching your friends the colours of the rainbow, then you would be the quasi-teacher.

That is the pretend-teacher, or the person who's acting as a teacher, even though you're not the real teacher. But still, you seem to know about indigo and orange and all the other colours, so keep playing teacher. You're doing a good job.

Quasi is plucked from Latin. It means **as if**. Staying overnight at your grandparents' house can be a quasi-holiday because things are so relaxing, their house a quasi-hotel. It's not a real hotel, of course, but sometimes quasi can be as good as the real thing.

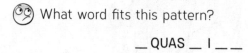 What word fits this pattern?

__ QUAS __ I __ __

Squashing

QUIDNUNC

[*KWID-nuhnk*]

Psst, what's the goss?

We know the type too well, that person with the biggest mouth, the keenest ears, ready to dish the latest furphy. (What, you don't know **furphy**? Then you're not reading this book in order. What a maverick you are! By the way, **maverick** is another word in this book. Under M.)

Let's return to **blabbermouths**, those people spreading stories all day, reporting on their nosy version of news. Stuff like:

Did you hear Ethan's sister loves Jacob from hockey?

We call such people gossips, or tattletales, or busybodies, or muckrakers. Another name is **QUIDNUNC**, which is odder and cooler. Pure Latin too, where *quid nunc* means **what now?**

Tell me the latest. What's happening now? I want more. What's going on?

Hearsay is another word for **rumour**, because rumours are stories we hear someone say. And that certain someone is a quidnunc.

A Spanish proverb, and a warning: Whoever gossips with you, will gossip about you.

RAMBUNCTIOUS
[*ram-BUHNGK-shuhs*]

My school principal loved to say **RAMBUNCTIOUS**. I think he liked its sound more than anything, its rhythm. Back then, I thought the word was a mix of naughty and noisy, because we were usually being naughty and noisy when he said it.

Not that **rambunctious** promised trouble for anybody. Mr Sharp called us **disrespectful** when he was really angry. **Rambunctious** was more like, 'Hey kids, settle down a bit. Deal?'

A mob of toddlers running loose in the library is rambunctious, though Mr Sharp might call them disrespectful, depending on his mood.

Rambunctious is rambunctious too, whacking together from several directions. The *ram* up-front is from the Vikings, the ancient warriors who called a fight a *rimma*. The *bunctious* bit is probably a rumbling of **bumptious**, an old-fashioned word for **rude**, with a bonus bump for extra sound FX.

 Q: Why are graveyards so noisy?

A: Because of the coffin.

RAZZMATAZZ

[RAZ-muh-TAZ]

In cartoons and comic strips, ZZZ means **sleep**. Which means **RAZZMATAZZ** has two short naps in one breath.

But don't be fooled, because razzmatazz is the opposite of going to sleep. It's more twist and shake, more songs and a double-decker cake – the stylish flipside of snoozing.

Razzle-dazzle is a close cousin, a flashy show of brilliance on the stage, on the sporting field, like the razzmatazz of a street parade or a dance routine, plenty of kicks and tricks, sparkle and glitter, the whole thing making your heart pitter-patter.

Nobody really knows how razzmatazz was born. The jazz slang was hatched in America, at a time when trombones and saxophones laced the air. Perhaps razzmatazz is just a crazy jazz rhyme, a double-rhyme in fact, to quicken the beat and capture the pizzazz.

Step up – eight dance-styles hide in each jumble below.

1. TONGA	2. BURMA	3. IS DOC?	4. UM, BAZ
5. WINGS	6. A LASS	7 CAN GO?	8. OK, PAL

1 tango, 2 rumba, 3 disco, 4 zumba, 5 swing, 6 salsa, 7 conga, 8 polka

RHOPALIC

[*ROH-par-lick*]

'I do not know where people believe exercise recharges.'

(That's a **RHOPALIC**, while this sentence you're reading isn't.)

Spot the difference? Take a closer look at the opening line about exercise to see if you can pinpoint its rarity. *I am the nerd which adores shaping fabulous rhopalics.* (Yes, that last sentence is one more rhopalic.) So what's a rhopalic and what's going on?

The secret lies in a Greek club. Not a nightclub, but a weapon a knight might carry around, walloping his enemies. **Club** in Greek is *rhopalon*, a tool that's narrow at the handle, getting thicker as you near the club's head. Picture a baseball bat made for clunking enemies.

Shape-wise, a rhopalic sentence does the same thing, starting off narrow then thickening with every word: *W is for wise women wading western wetlands willingly.* Count the letters and you'll see the pattern. It starts with a one-letter word, then a two-letter word, then three, four, five, and so on.

I am now very happy... Now it's your turn to shape some classy rhopalics

 Look, a rhopalic thriller in nine words:

I am all fear, going faster, running, escaping ferocious werewolves!

RISLEY

[*RIZZ-lee*]

If you have a beanbag at home, here's a challenge.

Take off your shoes. (No, that's not the challenge.) Now lie on the floor, the beanbag beside you. Next, raise your legs, feet together. Use your arms like props on your thighs if you like, just to keep your legs upright.

(Hang on – if you're doing that now, then how are you reading this book?)

Don't worry. Let's continue. If you can, bend your knees and put the beanbag on the soles of your feet, like lodging a fat marshmallow on a wobbly table.

Inch by inch, keeping the bag balanced on your feet, return your legs to their full height. Can you hold your position? Well done, you're almost there. Because the last challenge is to roll the bag in the air, using your feet to gently spin the marshmallow.

Do that – even after a few tries – and you've done a **RISLEY**, a **circus trick** named after American acrobat, Richard Risley Carlisle. He developed the stunt in the 1840s, twirling balls and volunteers with his feet. After beanbags, why not try your microwave?

 An acrobat like Richard Risley Carlisle would often wear a leotard, the gymnastic onesie named after Jules Leotard, a second acrobat honoured in the dictionary.

SENSUOUSNESS

[*SEN-sho-uss-nuhs*]

Sensuous is a sensuous word. Not just its silky sound, but the shape of each curvy S, every groovy U. Add NESS to the end and **SENSUOUSNESS** is one snaky delight.

Say it, if you don't believe me. *SEN-sho-uss-nuhs*.

If something is sensuous, it can be felt with feelings or fingertips. A sensuous song makes your skin tingle, your heart throb. It touches you. Or you can do the touching, running your hand along sensuous velvet, squeezing the plastic pimples of bubble wrap.

In Scrabble, a game that word nerds find sensuous, every letter in SENSUOUSNESS scores one point, which is sensational. In map-reading, S, E and N are all compass points, short for South, East and North. Take them away from SENSUOUSNESS and out comes an owl-howl – UOU!

So why give a hoot? That owly howl is a clue, a sound built to rebound left or right and spell the same thing – what we know is a palindrome.

Because here's the real magic. Spin SENSUOUSNESS into a circle and look what happens:

Q: Why can't you be rude to sandwiches?

A: Because they have fillings.

SHENANIGANS
[*shuh-NAN-i-guhns*]

Maybe a woman was selling candles in San Francisco, around 1850 or so. And one day, a boy walked past with a toy telescope. With the sun so bright, and the angle of the lens just right, a flash of glare made the candle-seller sneeze. '*Shhhhuh-nann-eeee-gunnnnhs*', she went, blowing out her whole shop.

To be honest, nobody knows if that's how **SHENANIGANS** was born, a quirky word for **prank-playing**, or **mucking around**. If that telescope kid was trying to make the woman sneeze, then he'd be doing some shenanigans. Or if I insist my candle story is true, then I'm guilty of shenanigans too.

Because maybe there's another story. The Irish word for **fox** is *sionnach*, which sounds like shenanigans, a shorter version. And we know that storybook foxes are always playing tricks, so maybe that's how shenanigans came to be.

In terms of spelling, shenanigans seems a cousin of hooligans, those tough-and-rumble ruffians with a talent for shenanigans. In fact, hooligans are the last sort of people to wear cardigans, unless they're up to no-good shenanigans.

 Shenanigans was a champion racehorse in America during the 1960s. Her grandfather **sire** was called Fighting Fox, while her mum – or **dam** – was named Bold Irish.

SKULDUGGERY

[*skuhl-DUHG-uh-ree*]

It's eerie to imagine bones, shovels, worms...

Those are the pictures that spring to mind when I hear **SKULDUGGERY**, a word ready-made for graves and shadowy figures.

Spooky to the marrow, those images aren't too far wrong, either. Skulduggery has that power. You probably don't need me to explain what it means, but the publisher says I have to.

Think shenanigans, just like our last word, but ten times creepier. Anything **secretive**, anything **dishonest** or against the rules, lies at the heart of skulduggery.

Tombs and skulls seem buried in the syllables, but that can't be proven. Skulduggery is a murky word, both what it means as well as the mystery of its history. Deep down, there's no denying it: skulduggery is one more word I love, but not a word I trust.

Q: What happens when a ghost gets lost in the fog?

A: They're mist

SMOOT

[*SMOOT*]

How tall are you? Do you know to the last millimetre?

Most kids do. As you grow taller, it's exciting to see how far you stretch with every passing year. And for any reader who's **170 centimetres** tall, congratulations. You are a **SMOOT**.

The word comes from Oliver Smoot, a young university student who was exactly that tall. Well, that short, because Ollie was chosen by his friends to be a ruler.

Not a monarch, but a measuring stick. In 1958, Ollie and his friends had to measure Harvard Bridge, a long flat road stretching over the Charles River in Boston.

Forget inches. Who cared about metres? These students preferred to measure in smoots, as Ollie lay flat and his friends marked each body-length in chalk, one Smoot by the next Smoot.

After a while, getting tired from so much standing-then-lying, Ollie let his mates lift and carry him, laying him down like a human ruler. For the record, Harvard Bridge is 364.4 smoots (and one ear).

 Other rough measures include an arm's length, a hair's breadth, a whisker, a nose (for horse races), a football field (for hectares) and an Olympic pool – or Sydney Harbour – for litres.

STOIC
[STOH-ick]

There's a bucket of cold water on the table. It's *freeeeeeezing*, a word which seems chillier the more Es you add. So cold it's almost ice.

Now put your hand in. Go on, dare you. Put it in the water and keep it there.

Not so keen now, are you? Here, let me go first. That's only fair.

'Mm-nnhh, that's pleasant. Aaaah, yes, so refreshing, this water. That's mmmn-hhh, that's why I'm nnrhh-nggh, why I'm leaving my hand there, just to enjoy the cool.'

Can you tell I'm lying? My mm-nnhhhs gave it away. So do my nnrhh-ngghs. If you want the truth, this water is agony and I'm removing my hand before it falls off.

Yet if I was **STOIC**, you wouldn't hear a single mmmh-nggh. Not a peep. That's because stoic people can suffer pain in silence, **showing no emotions**. No sighs or frowns, but rather as calm as a stone.

The word is plucked from Greek where *stoïkos* describes **a porch**, the shady front of a temple. This was where students met thousands of years ago to study the art of accepting life for what it is, even if it's freeeeezing.

Be careful with stoic. It doesn't rhyme with **hoick**, a slang word for **throw**. To help you remember: a true stoic is heroic.

SUBITISE

[SUB-uh-tise, or SOO-bi-tise or even suh-BYE-tise!]

Glance at the turnips below and tell me how many you see. If you said five, without touching each turnip with your finger, then you can **SUBITISE**.

Subitising is counting minus the counting. Instead of going one-two-three, your brain does the one-two-three for you. Or five, in the case of turnips. Now see how you go with wombats.

Wombats are harder. Not because they're wombats but because there are more to count. If you said nine without too much thinking, then you're a super subitiser. But I bet most of you needed to count the marsupials to make sure.

Subitise comes from *subitus* in Latin, a word for **speedy**. Jean Piaget, the Swiss doctor to coin the word, loved to measure how some infants had the knack to **count in a flash**, while others did not. As a rule, the better you are at maths, the more wombats you can muster in a jiffy. Me? I'm a crummy subitiser, except when it comes to letters.

Jackhammer, for example, has ten letters. I knew that straight away. Did you? And ten is the same quantity as fingers we have on both hands. Wait, let me check.

See if you can subitise each line of lamps below. How many did you magically count correctly?

SUPERCILIOUS

(soo-per-SIL-ee-uhs)

Seagulls have no eyebrows. Ever notice that? Squinching their feathers, tilting their beaks, gulls can't be **SUPERCILIOUS**, not if we're being fussy about words.

Supercilious means **smug** or **proud**. A supercilious passenger treats everyone on the bus like dirt, the driver included. To a supercilious person, the bus would seem like their own limousine, all other passengers nothing but grubby stowaways.

Pulling SUPERICILIOUS into pieces, the *super* part is easy. That means **higher**, like superheroes or Superman, characters who never catch buses. Then there's *cilious*, Part two of the word, which links to *cilia* in Latin, the name for **eyebrow**.

If you want to be supercilious, curl your eyebrows. Go on. Make them lift in the mirror as if you know everything there is to know. See, now that's supercilious, another word for **snobby** or **superior**.

Seagulls can't do that, even though they act smug. They have the attitude, just not the eyebrows.

 How I enjoy a luscious mango. But can you take LUSCIOUS out of SUPERCILIOUS, then mix the leftovers to describe the perfect mango?

Ripe

TABOO
[tuh-BOO]

Public pools are full of rules. No diving, no bombing. No boogie boards, no boogies.

You can't eat in the pool, or suck lollies, or use water pistols. You can't play a banjo in the shallow end. You can't play Nintendo in the deep end either. In fact, banjos and Nintendo are **TABOO** at my local pool, along with underwater cameras and hair dye.

Taboo comes from Tahiti, a tiny Pacific island where *tapu* means **forbidden. Not allowed. Not happening**. New Zealand's Maori people use the same word. *Tapu* describes any action that's forbidden, like eating holy food or spying on a secret ceremony.

Captain Cook was the first Englishman to hear of taboo, exploring the Pacific in 1770 and learning about the no-nos of Pago Pago. Village elders knew the rules – they still do – reminding everyone there's no pushing, no running, no undies as cozzies and definitely no lawnmowers in the kiddies' pool.

My pool tried to type a taboo, but every letter moved one forward (or one back) in the alphabet. What is the true taboo?

MP   QTCAFS   SBEUT   JO   CHUJOH   ONPK

No rubber rafts in diving pool.

TEMPLOID

[*TEM-ployd*]

When people wear shorts or skirts, resting their flesh against grass and furniture, they are sure to get a **TEMPLOID**.

You might have one now, if you've been sitting since AMBIDEXTROUS, or GROAK at least. Take a look. See if you can find **a dent on your skin**. Maybe it's a woven pattern from the chair, or a red groove on your arm from where you've been leaning all this time. Each impression is a temploid, a brief tattoo of touch.

My grandma had a wicker chair in her sunroom. The chair was deep and woven together by willow strands. That's where I loved to daydream, leaving temploids on my arms and legs like phantom crosswords with no answers.

Temploid comes from *templum*, **a long wooden beam below a roof**. The same beam was part of a weaving machine called a **loom**, a gizmo designed to turn threads into rugs and carpets.

Quite a lot of work compared to lounging in the grass. Who needs a loom when the weeds and stalks do all the work, imprinting a temploid on your leg?

Speaking of patterns, name at least three words with this pattern:

_ _ S K I N _

Basking, busking, masking, risking, tasking

TOADY

[TOE-dee]

Four hundred years ago, carnivals went from town to town. Like a circus minus a tent, a funfair without a rollercoaster.

Kids could hop on ponies or ride slides on old sacks. Adults could get their fortunes told or buy a bottle of miracle medicine. One spoonful and this potion might heal wounds, restore sight, do anything at all, if you believed the doctor.

Doctor? Hah! More a performer pretending to be a doctor, selling his fakery to make big money.

To con the crowd, the so-called doctor had a helper. Man or woman, it didn't matter, so long as this helper swallowed a toad. You heard me. *Swallowed a toad*.

Toads are poisonous. If you want to live a long life, don't lick hair dryers or swallow toads. But if you're a **TOADY** – short for **toad-eater** – then you do what you're told. A **crawler**, a big suck, you follow instructions, even if instructed to pop a toad in your mouth, warts and all.

By magic, the potion would save the toad-eater, as the helper was called at first. Suckers started digging in their pockets, convinced the medicine was real. Next week, by the time they realised the potion was fiction, the toad-swallowing show had jumped town.

 Q: What did the frog say as he looked through the books at the library?

TRIAGE

[TREE-ahzh]

Your climb a tree. And then you fall from the tree. Thud. Ouch. Your ankle is broken.

An ambulance comes. You go to hospital in a loud hurry. The emergency room is packed because half the town has been clumsy or unlucky that day, needing help with burnt fingers, spider bites or all sorts of cuts and scrapes.

The nurse in charge needs to juggle. Not balls but patients. He needs to decide who needs help soonest.

Just because a kid with pepper in her eye was first to arrive doesn't matter in the long run. Pepper in the eye is annoying, but not as bad as a broken ankle.

Deciding which injury needs the quickest attention is called **TRIAGE**, sorting out what needs fixing first.

In French, *trier* means **to sift**, like sifting mud to find gold. In his mind, the triage nurse is sifting patients, shaking them in his brain to single out the biggest emergency. So far your broken ankle wins the triage race. But if someone arrives with *two* broken ankles, or perhaps a python wrapped around their neck, you'll be sifted down the list.

Eight people complain about pain, each one using a different word below. Can you sift the list like a triage nurse, ordering the worst pain to the least pain?

achy

burning

excruciating

intense

mild

nagging

sharp

shooting

Try this list with friends and see if you agree with your triage.

TRIANTIWONTYGONG

[*tri-ANT-ee-WONN-tee-gong*]

The monster goes by many names. Perth kids could be haunted by the **TRIANTIWONTYGONG**, a creepy cousin of the bunyip that lives in sewers or billabongs.

Meanwhile, boys and girls in South Australia could become supper for **triantiwontigalope**, or the **triantimontygoggle**.

In the meantime, Brisbane babies who crawl the bush after dark might become sweet-and-sour snacks for the **triantegowontegong**.

For once, the spelling doesn't matter. Nor does the way you say it. So long as kids settle for staying home at night, tucked up snug in bed.

That's the plan behind the triantiwontygong – the creature's most common name. The **monster** is a myth, a fib with sixteen letters. Adults invented the baby-muncher to spook their sons and daughters, just as ogres in fairy tales make us cling tighter to our pillows.

A poet called Clarence James Dennis – better known as CJ – invented one version of the beast in 1921, thanks to his poem 'The Triantiwontigongolope'. Yet CJ's creature was a bug, not a bunyip. As he put it, 'There's a very funny insect that you do not often spy, and it isn't quite a spider, and it isn't quite a fly...' Not as terrifying, but still another reason to stay under the doona.

 Q: Do monsters eat popcorn with their fingers?

A: No, they eat the fingers separately

ULLAGE

[*ULL–ij*]

Do me a favour and pour a glass of milk. When did you stop? Halfway up the glass or near the top?

If you went too far, get a sponge. There's no point crying over spilt milk – just mop it up. But I'm guessing you're too smart for that rookie error.

Hours of practice teaches our glass-pouring brains when enough is enough and we learn to un-tilt the carton in time. That's why humans have pet cats instead of cats having pet humans, because cats can't grasp the carton arts.

Wait, before you drink the milk, I have one more favour to ask. Exactly how far is the milk's surface from the glass's lip? Two centimetres? Three? I'll guess four, as that's the average **ULLAGE**.

Ullage is **the gap between liquid and the container's top**. Non-thirsty people are happy with a big ullage, with far less water in the bottle. Or milk in the glass.

Ullage comes from old French, where *aouiller* means **to fill a wine cask**. The word relates to *oeil*, a French **eye**, and the origin of our English **hole**.

Makes sense, really. Thirsty people have a colossal hole in their stomachs, like an inner ullage that needs a long glass of milk to fill.

What sealed drink container, when sitting inside a large tub-like container, spells a six-letter word for **empty**?

ULULATE

[*YOOL-yuh-layt*]

After three – one, two, three: 'Arrrrooooooooooo!'
   That's how you **ULULATE**, meaning **to howl like a wolf**.

In some countries, when a coffin is carried through the town, you can pay people to ululate, making the sad day sound sadder. And noisier.

Ululation is natural in the wild, the chorus of jackals and hyenas, as one pack signals to another pack, or a lone wolf looks for a wolf-mate.

Dogs do it too. When one pooch starts to ululate, they all go berserk, turning your suburb into one big coyote choir, each dog saying, 'I'm here tooooooooo!'

Armed with spears, a warrior might ululate before risking the battlefield – an old trick to find your courage, to summon your inner animal. Raucous, but with good reason. That's why many a gladiator was a ululator.

Reread this page and you will find another word that also starts with a repeated pair of letters, just like ululate. What is it?

UMAMI
[*oo-MAH-me*]

Dare you to lick a slippery dip. The bottom or the top – you choose. Or maybe the rail where you put your hand. Give it a lick. Lick the lot and tell me what you taste.

(Note: would you lick a slippery dip if your best friend dared you? Probably not. So why lick a slide if a writer called David dared you? That'd be ludicrous.)

But if you *did* lick the metal, then your tongue might taste salt (from sweaty kids), or sweet (from melted gelato), or sour (from kids throwing up their gelato)...

Or maybe **UMAMI**, the secret sensation hiding among your taste buds. For years, whether eating popcorn or pumpkin, we have put taste in four boxes – sweet, sour, salty, bitter.

Until Kikunae Ikeda came along, a hundred years ago. This chemist discovered umami, a **pleasant savoury taste** in his own Japanese language. Umami lurks in mushrooms and prawns and milk, even some dips – except for slippery dips.

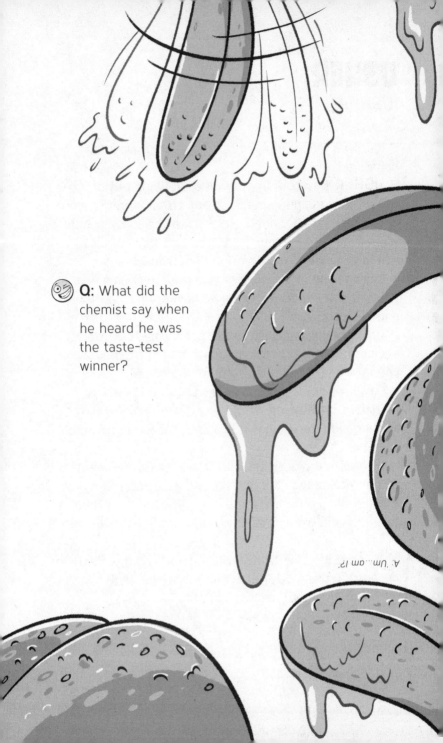

Q: What did the chemist say when he heard he was the taste-test winner?

A: Um...am I?

USHER

[USH-uh]

If teachers teach, and painters paint, then why don't ushers ush?

USHER was born in old Rome, stepping out of *ostiarius*, the Latin name for **door**. Ushers tend to work at the movies, checking tickets or waving torches, telling you where to park your bum. Now and then they tell you stop talking, turning ushers into shushers.

Outside the cinema, ushers can lurk in churches or palaces, a team of dainty servants with brass buttons and a seat-map.

Girl ushers were once called usherettes, but everyone decided that an usher is an usher, male or female, young or old. So why use a different word?

Call it ridiculous, but the reason I love USHER is thanks to **crumbling**. That's when you break a word into smaller pieces, like snapping a chocolate bar into squares.

Broken into pieces, USHERED is a treasure trove. You can make US and SHE and HE and HER and HERE and ERE (an old word meaning before) and RED. Truth be told, I have a word-nerd crush on usher.

Triple the D in USHERED, and you can mix the nine new letters – USHEREDDD – into one word? As a clue, the word means wobbled.

VELLEITY

(vuh-LEE-et-tee)

VELLEITY is a shallow valley.

No, it's not. But it is a word, I promise. Unless you think velleity is the book's final fake. Which maybe it is. Who am I to ruin your guessing game? Or maybe you believe you've found the fakes already...

Instead of a valley, velleity is a desire, but a faint one. Imagine you want kiwifruit on your porridge. Yet that would mean peeling the kiwis – the fruit, not the birds. But you're feeling too lazy, so you eat your porridge bare – the porridge, not you.

This is velleity, a wish too weak to act upon. More like a half-idea, a feeble urge. The word comes from Latin, where *velle* means **willing**. But not willing enough in this case.

And if velleity *is* the book's last fake, why not check a dictionary? Well, you could, but that would mean leaving your chair or bed, or visiting the library, or turning on your computer. And since your bug to know is a velleity, you don't budge.

VELLEITY hides EYE, a word that reads the same either way. Not counting LIL, slang for little, what two more palindrome words hide in VELLEITY?

Eve, level

VOMITORIUM
(vom-i-TAWR-ee-uhm)

Ever been to a stadium to see a major sporting match? Or maybe you went to see a ballet show, or a concert in a large theatre?

If you did, then you've used a **VOMITORIUM** without ever being sick. Remarkable, but how did you do it?

The reason gets down to *vomere*, a Latin word for **spew out**, just like shaken cola spews from a bottle, or rainwater gushes from a pipe, or, yes, okay, alright-alright, a seasick passenger can, well, *vomere* too.

But instead of rainwater or fizzy drink or chewed-up carrots, the spewing action in vomitorium describes how big crowds move. When people are crammed tight in one space, seeing a show or a game, you need wide passages to help everybody exit, to spew from the stadium onto the street.

Just like you need wide passages for everyone to enter as well, to spew into their seats minus the mess. Together these passages are called **vomitoria** – that's the plural – without a single icky puddle of half-chewed broccoli to be seen. Or smelt.

Q: What do you call a tub full of vomit?

A: A barf

VUVUZELA

[*voo-voo-ZELL-ah*]

Say *vu-vu*. Say it again. Now say it louder, faster, and keep on *vu-vuing* until your lips go numb.

Do it with friends and you'll sound like a bee swarm. To boost the noise, do it with long plastic horns, *vu-vuing* at the narrow end, and you'll resemble bees in stereo.

The din is too deafening for a football game. Over in South Africa, where sports fans go *vu-vu* in the sun, players on the ground struggle to hear the referee's whistle. Which is why some people tried to ban the **VUVUZELA** – the plastic horn so popular in the stadiums.

The word comes from Zulu, which is neat because ZULU the language hides in VUVUZELA the word. Translated, it means **going vu-vu**, the word an echo of the trumpet's buzz.

Long before plastic came along, vuvuzelas were made of antelope horns. Yes, a horn from a horn. One antelope – the kudu – has a twisty, hollow horn that's ideal for making a buzzy trumpet. Try saying that in a tongue-twisty way: *Who knew Zulus blew vu-vu on new kudu vuvuzelas?*

 Q: What do you call a horn that's sweet to eat?

WOOZLE

[*WOO-zuhl*]

The **WOOZLE** resembles the weasel. It lives in cold places and loves heavy snow.

Winnie-the-Pooh and his best friend Piglet know this. That's why they go woozle-hunting when the snow cloaks the trees in One Hundred Acre Wood.

The creature doesn't really exist. The writer AA Milne just dreamt up the woozle – but Pooh and Piglet don't know that. In fact, they don't even know that they're dreamt as well.

Anyhow, one cold day Pooh and Piglet marched around a clump of larch trees, hoping to catch a woozle snoozing.

What they find are footprints, two sets in the snow, both heading the same way as the hunters. Pooh and Piglet keep going in circles. And the more laps they do, the more prints they find.

The prints are their own, of course. And that's why a woozle is not just a **make-believe** monster, but any strange fact you're hoping to prove – like the moon being made of cheese – and the only proof you find is **bogus**. Not just bogus, but dreamt up by other searchers, on purpose or by accident. Only smart people can tell real things from woozles.

The woozle might be imaginary, but can you find a real animal, a real animal address plus a real animal product, using the letters of WOOZLE each time?

Owl, zoo, wool.

WUG

[*WUG*]

This is a **WUG**. *Now there is another one. There are two of them. There are two* _ _ _ _. (*Can you guess what word fills the blank?*)

Jean Gleason was the principal wug-maker. The American professor drew her wug sixty years ago, then sketched a second to see how well a child knew English. Jean called it the Wug Test, inventing her fluff-balls to test if kids could turn one wug into two wugs by adding S to the tail.

Wugs, like woozles, don't really exist, of course, unless pictures count. Jean chose the name because it was odd, but not so odd that a wug couldn't obey the rules of language.

When not wugging, Professor Gleason made other cool sentences. See how well your brain knows English by filling in Jean's blanks:

A man who ZIBS is a _ _ _ _ _ _ _.

This is a dog with QUIRKS on him. He is all covered in QUIRKS. What kind of a dog is he? He is a _ _ _ _ _ _ _ *dog.*

This is a girl who knows how to SPOW. She is SPOWING. She did the same thing yesterday. What did she do yesterday? Yesterday she _ _ _ _ _ _ _.

Zibber, Quirky, Spowed

Dog ➜ dogs. Wug ➜ wugs. Most English words gain an S when going from one to more than one. But what noun on this page doesn't follow that rule?

Child

XEROX

[*ZEER-ocks*]

Can I confess something? I didn't write this page.

Instead, I found a fantastic book in the library that talked about brand names and I copied the page on the **photocopy** machine.

Gotcha. That's a fib – and a crime, copying someone's writing to pretend it's yours. You know this is me writing, don't you? Can't you tell? I'd never **XEROX** another book to say it's mine. As if.

But Xerox is a brand, a company that makes photocopiers. They started sixty years ago, using light and toner and electric currents to clone any page. In science this is called **xerography** – or **dry-picturing** in Greek.

Joseph Wilson, the company's founder, thought X looked so stylish he copied half the word to spell his brand. Pretty soon, as more copiers copied Xerox machines, people started using the brand as a word, the X slowly shrinking, and dictionaries copied that trend.

Last, just to prove I wrote this page, my middle name is Robert and I wear size 11 shoes. No one else could possibly know that. Except my mum, and she didn't write it.

TUTU, the ballerina skirt, is a copycat word, where TU does a double act. All your next answers fall into the same Xerox box.

1. Mistake (6)

2. Farewell (3-3)

3. Cheerleader's ball (6)

4. Quickly! (4,4!)

5. Whisper (6)

6. Christmas cracker (6)

7. Pop Lady (4)

8. Kindie whiz? (3-3)

9. Crushed wheat (8)

10. Minigolf (4-4)

1. booboo. 2 bye-bye. 3 pompom. 4 chop chop! 5 murmur. 6 bonbon. 7 Gaga. 8 pee-pee. 9 couscous. 10 putt-putt

YARG
[YAAARG]

Sounds like a crow but comes from a cow – that's **YARG**.

This creamy, **crumbly cheese** must sleep in a dark room before it's ready to eat, wrapped in nettle leaves for extra flavour.

Yarg is made in Cornwall, the bottom left corner of England. The peculiar name is due to Alan and Jenny Gray. A few years ago, the farming couple found the cheese recipe in an old book, dating back four centuries, and decided to make it for fun.

So did you notice that surname? Now turn Gray the other way. Hooray, you saved the day, making your own yarg, and discovering the very reason the cheese owns that outrageous name.

Imagine if other inventions were named after inventors in reverse. Ford cars would be Drof cars. Dunlop tyres would be Polnuds. Or the lightbulb, invented by Thomas Edison, would turn into a noside.

 If yarg is cheese named after its maker turned backwards, then Edam is the Dutch cheese that's made backwards!

YORKIPOO

[*YAW-kee-poo*]

Tim was a labrador-something. We never knew exactly and Tim didn't tell us. His head and snout were pure labrador, while his skinny hips belonged to a kelpie or a pointer.

Maybe our pet was a kelpador? A labointer?

Welcome to the world of **designer dogs**, though Tim was really a mutt, his mum and dad a chance meeting.

Unlike other pets, where breeders mix dogs to make a fetching blend, whether that blend fetches or not. Tim did. He was a great fetcher. I bet you the **YORKIPOO** would hesitate if you threw a tennis ball. Not Tim. He'd hurtle until that ball was in his jaws.

Smallish and fluffy, the yorkipoo is the pup to come from a **Yorkshire terrier** and a **toy poodle** getting together. Not a real toy, but a mini-version of the usual poodle.

Yorkipoos are loyal. They don't lose hair, like labradors do, or labrador-somethings. And if their cuteness doesn't warm your heart, then at least yorkipoo the word will always make you smile.

 Q: What do you get when you cross a cocker spaniel, a poodle, and a rooster?

A: A cockerpoodledoo.

ZHOOSH

[ZUSH – rhymes with push]

ZHOOSH sounds like a toboggan sliding through soft snow. But it's more like fingers sliding through your hair.

Zhooshing is the studio knack of **making things fresher**, more eye-catching. The word comes from actors' slang in London, via the Romani people who say *yusher* to mean **clean**.

Adding more colour to your drawing can do the trick, just like a pinch of spice can zhoosh a meal. A little splash of make-up can improve your dress-up costume, all in the name of zhooshing.

Oxford Dictionary, one of the most reputable in the world, is shaky about how to spell zhoosh. This often happens when words seem like sound effects, or words come from other languages.

On top of zhoosh, the *Oxford* also has zhush, joozh, zoozh and zhuzh. Something tells me those Oxford people need to zhoosh their Z section.

Zillionth starts with Z and ends with H, just like zhoosh. What slang word for **nothing** can say the same?

Zilch

ZUGZWANG

[*TSOOK-zvang*]

Your rubber raft is sinking. Water gushes through a big rip in the floor, too big to patch, and too much water to stay afloat.

You need to make a choice, as crocodiles start to circle. Or wait, maybe they're alligators. As if that matters now! Either way, their teeth are sharp and your raft is sinking.

a) Do you risk the river and those gator-crocs? Or:

b) Do you paddle for the jungle on the bank, knowing the jungle teems with snakes and jaguars?

Like it or not, this little pickle is called a **ZUGZWANG**.

The word comes from chess. *Zug* is the German for **move**, as well as **train**, because trains move, as well as moving people.

Zwang means **force**. Not the police, but the pressure – just like your raft adventure is forcing you to move, even if you'd rather stay still and pretend your problem isn't happening.

Chess players fall into zugzwang when they need to move a piece, even if harm will come their way, no matter which way they pick. Move left, move right – damage is coming. Move up, move down – your situation will only weaken. Regardless of your *Zug*, a zig or zag will only zap.

In Arabic, *shah-mat* means 'the king died'. Say the phrase a few times and you'll hear another chess predicament – checkmate, where your king is doomed to die. (Sorry for giving this fun book such a grim end – but I was zugzwanged by the alphabet!)

Who dunny? Did you pick the fakes from the flock?

Welcome, Detective [your surname here]. Here's the page where you find out which three words are fake.

Or maybe you don't like guessing games, so you came straight here, desperate to remove the mystery.

Either way, you've arrived at the right place. Though rather than listing the made-up words, I've used a little number trick. That way, if anyone stumbles across this page too soon, then the fun won't be spoilt by seeing the fakes in a list.

To unmask each phony hiding in the book, just solve the simple maths below. (If you need help, then it's okay to ask Mum or Dad.) Each answer will be the page number where the fake word is pretending to be real.

Deep breath, here we go.

FAKE WORD 1 = 2 + 5 + 9 – 12
FAKE WORD 2 = 67 – 16
FAKE WORD 3 = 40 + 28 + 19 + 22

Packed with word puzzles, tongue twisters and brain teasers, *WORDBURGER* has all the ingredients you need to solve cryptic crosswords. Word wizard David Astle will teach you the different kinds of wordplay – anagrams, pangrams, spoonerisms, tongue-twisters, homophones – before presenting you with crossword puzzles to solve using all the tactics you've learnt so far.

It's the word nerd's bible of wordy trickery!

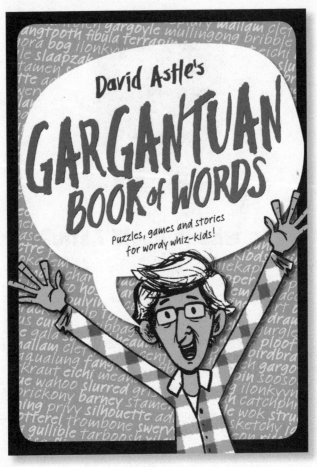

David Astle's *Gargantuan Book of Words* is one ginormous
storehouse of stories and puzzles, quizzes and riddles, mazes and
codes, games and lists – all about words. From Oops-A-Doozy
to Yuckarama, you will meet funny goldfish names, surfie slang,
African idiom, pirate maps, word-bracelets and oodles
of other language delights, with ample puzzles to crack,
riddles to guess and wordy trivia to gobble. If you have
a gigantic appetite for words, big or small,
Gargantuan is your ideal feast.

photo by Michele Ransom-Hughes

So who is David Astle?

David Astle loves words. Eats them. Dreams them. Not just their meaning but their shape and sound, the stories they whisper, the power they hold, their mystery and mastery, plus the fun they promise.

That's why he makes puzzles for newspapers, and for kids as well. It's also why he writes books, sharing his alphabet love in *Gargantuan* and *Wordburger* for kids, plus *Puzzled*, *Cluetopia*, *Riddledom*, *Rewording the Brain* for grown-ups.

David's Wordplay column appears in the *Sydney Morning Herald*, looking at language from every angle. Meanwhile, on TV you can catch him unpeeling English on ABC's *News Breakfast*, or co-hosting *Letters and Numbers*, an SBS gameshow that spins words every weeknight.

So it's just as well David loves words – he grabs every chance to play with them.

www.davidastle.com